SO-BIO-387

ARKANA

KARMA AND DESTINY IN THE I CHING

Guy Damian-Knight was born in Nicosia, Cyprus, but has lived for most of his life in the United Kingdom. He studied law at the University of Kent and is a member of the Honorary Society of Middle Temple. Besides a long-standing passion for Eastern religious thought, his interests also include film and music, and politics and economics. He is author of *The I Ching on Love* (Blandford Press, 1984) and *The I Ching on Business and Decision Making* (Rider, 1986). He is continuing his investigations into the *I Ching* as they pertain to logic, intelligence and unitive knowledge.

GUY DAMIAN-KNIGHT

KARMA AND DESTINY IN THE I CHING

ARKANA

LONDON AND NEW YORK

First published in 1987 by Arkana
(Routledge & Kegan Paul Ltd)

11 New Fetter Lane, London EC4P 4EE

Published in the USA by
Routledge & Kegan Paul Inc.
in association with Methuen Inc.
29 West Street 35th Street, New York, NY 10001

Set in Sabon, 10 on 11 pt.
by Columns of Reading
and printed in the British Isles
by The Guernsey Press Co. Ltd.
Guernsey, Channel Islands

© Guy Damian-Knight 1987

The mathematical re-evaluation of the
I Ching, as it is used in this work,
is specifically protected by Copyright.

No part of this book may be reproduced in
any form without permission from the publisher
except for the quotation of brief passages
in criticism

Library of Congress Cataloging in Publication Data

Damian-Knight, Guy.
Karma and destiny in the I ching.

Bibliography: p.
1. Divination. 2. Karma. 3. I ching. I. Title.
BF1773.D36 1987   133.3'3   86-17491

British Library CIP Data also available

ISBN 1-85063-038-0

For Ludwig,
with love and thanks
for all your help and kindness
over many years

The wheel has come full circle. I am here.

Merlyn
from *The Book of Merlyn*,
by T.H. White

ACKNOWLEDGMENTS

The author would like to thank Penguin for permission to reproduce selected passages from Rainer Maria Rilke, *Selected Poems*, 1969.

CONTENTS

INTRODUCTION

The destinies of men are subject to immutable laws that
must fulfil themselves. But man has it in his power to
shape his fate [decide on the quality with which his actions
shall be invested, effort of the will/consciousness] according as his behaviour exposes him to the influence of
benevolent or destructive forces.

Hexagram 15, the *I Ching*,
Wilhelm translation

This book is essentially intended to be a work of guidance.
From its inception, I have kept to the view that the most useful
form a book about Tao and Karma can take (for those who
relate to the matter seriously) is to produce, as the *I Ching*
does, *frames of action*, or in this case Karmic pictures. These
Karmic pictures are set out under the heading 'Karmic
numbers' (1–31), which correspond to the hexagrams of the *I
Ching*. They describe landscapes of thought, emotion and
action, embracing both the physical and spiritual spheres, by
which the 'Karmic Traveller' may attempt to orientate his life
on the journey of Illumination.

At the end of this Introduction I describe how it is possible to
achieve this through a wholly consistent mathematical arrangement of the content and structure of the traditional *I Ching*. I
have tried to keep these explanations simple and to spare the
reader unnecessary argument in order that the purpose and
usefulness of the information provided is kept before him.
Clearly, however, it is also necessary to reveal something of the
'architecture of thought' on which this work is based.

It is, without doubt, possible to redefine the fundamental
truths, life and nature of that body of wisdom we call Taoist
thought and discover within the existing form of the *I Ching*

other possible structures and inter-relationships which lend themselves to its intelligent rearrangement. I shall not explore here the possible parallels with or rationalisations of the mathematical basis of the *I Ching*, but only state that the six levels which are pictured with deceptive simplicity in the two-dimensional hexagrams are a Universal. They are to be found in the structures of consciousness delineated by other ancient traditions, notably Buddhism and Vedanta, and later by G.I. Gurdjieff, P.D. Ouspensky and the Theosophists, among others. More recently this six-dimensional parallel is reflected by psychologist Timothy Leary in his theory of 'evolutionary spirals' (*ref. Exo Psychology*) and in the six stages of evolution presented by Ken Wilber in *A Sociable God*.* According to the latter these are:- 1) the physical level, 2) the emotional level, 3) the mental level, 4) the psychic level, 5) the subtle level and 6) the causal level.

Undoubtedly in time to come, and once they have been proved scientifically, the parallels between the mathematical architecture of the *I Ching* and Nature will startle both philosophers and scientists. Fritjof Capra's *Tao of Physics* already points the way. But I am concerned merely to produce a work which may be used as a direct guide to the Taoist system of Karma.

I do not wish to avoid the complex philosophical implications raised by this treatment of the ideas of Karma and Destiny, but to confront them head-on in analytical onslaught would only achieve a 'picture of a picture of a picture'. Therefore, instead of mere intellectual speculation, I prefer to resolve these issues by presenting a completely consistent system which can account for the dynamics in which our lives are actually involved. I am astonished and delighted by the fact that this Karmic system is immanent and innate to the Taoist world view, and has always been present within it since the *I Ching* was first constructed as a mirror for the Changes. All that remained to be done so far as the rationalisation of Karma and Destiny were concerned, was to discover, according to natural law, how the mathematical information was to be

---

* This has by no means been established. It is at this stage merely a contention of mine.

arranged or rearranged, in order to yield this hidden knowledge and realise it in the most practical and useful way.*

The *I Ching* is a gateway to the wide-open mysteries of the universe, and:

> The holy sages were possessed of this knowledge. They withdrew into seclusion and cultivated the spirit, so that they were able to penetrate the minds of all men, so that they could determine good fortune and misfortune [the frame or field of action], and so that they knew the past and the future (Settlement of Doubts). They could do this thanks to their reason and clearmindedness, their knowledge and their wisdom (determination of the field of action) and their divine power (Settlement of Doubts). This divine power to battle acts without weakening itself.
>
> *The Great Treatise*, Book Two, the *I Ching*
> Wilhelm translation

> Then death, so call'd, is but old matter dress'd
> In some new figure, and varied vest:
> Thus all things are but alter'd, nothing dies;
> And here and there the unbodied spirit flies . . .

---

* Conceived as a double-helix (an interlocking spiral) it is important to point out that the mathematical re-evaluation presented in this work represents *only one* of its two strands. The complementary strand must be set forth in a later work. This complementary strand deals with the empathic relations between people. This is properly the theme of Book Two in the traditional rendering of the *I Ching*. Book Two would deal with empathy.

The Karmic progressions pertaining to the way in which the individual establishes relationships and interacts with others, i.e. Karma and Empathy, are contained in the secondary cycle depicted in the *I Ching* in hexagrams 32 through to 64. This book does not deal with the progressions for Karma and Empathy but only with those for Karma and Destiny. However, the Karma and Empathy progressions are based on exactly the same series of mathematical derivations which form the structure of this book and contain six further Karmic pictures (making a total of twelve) representing the full inner and outer relationship of the individual to himself and to the world about him. Taken together they still represent only the 'Macro-cycle' (see Karmic numbers below).

It is my contention that we may well be looking at the actual evolutionary matrix of the human nervous system and human consciousness. This is something which will be explored more fully elsewhere. If this is right, the implications are clearly of great significance.

From tenement to tenement though toss'd,
The soul is still the source, the same, the figure only lost:
And as the soften'd wax new seals receives,
This face assumes and that impression leaves;
Now call'd by one, now by another name;
The form is only changed, the wax is still the same.
So death, so call'd, can but the form deface,
The immortal flies out in empty space;
To seek her fortune in some other place . . .

Ovid's *Metamorphoses*
(The John Dryden translation)

PART ONE

Fate

Whatever an individual's intellectual stance on the idea of Fate, it has never, historically, been regarded as a totally fanciful notion. Whether one chooses to believe, or not, that we are in some curious way fated, must depend to some degree on personal experience, and the way in which one has been conditioned. Certainly it is not enough for exponents of the 'do or die' philosophy, proud pragmatists, hard-nosed rationalists or realists glibly to deny such a concept. Neither is it accurate to equate a belief in or an understanding of Fate with 'being a fatalist', i.e. one who denies personal responsibility for actions or for the consequences arising from events; in other words, the view that 'There was nothing I could have done about it, it was fated to happen.' Yet at one time or another all of us have felt that way, and in the final analysis it is hard to assess whether or not we were mistaken in that view. It is therefore difficult to be objective, let alone conclusive, about when individuals are free to act, and when they are not, especially for those who have experienced being led or driven by some higher will.

People hold, in general, one of four relationships with the question of Fate or 'No Fate':

(i) One is the totally fatalistic, i.e. 'there is no free will, only the *illusion* of free will'; 'just because we can't see the puppet strings doesn't mean they aren't there'.

(ii) There is no such force as Fate; there are no invisible strings which guide our actions; there is no 'divinity which shapes our ends'; we are 100 per cent responsible for each and every action, and consequently, each and every reaction arising from our actions during the course of our lives. The life is measured in action alone – no mystery.

Those who hold this position are often anti-religionists or atheists. These are the hard-nosed pragmatists mentioned earlier, or if not, alas, they live in despair.

(iii) The majority of people, however, do not fall wholly on one side or the other of that clear line, Fate/no Fate. They feel that in *some* things we are fated, but in others we have the responsibility to act appropriately, 'as the circumstances demand'. It is impossible to define more closely the myriad judgments and opinions of this large section of the population as such definition would need to depend on so many variables: intuition, mood and belief, which do not yield to scientific investigation. Certainly, of the three views so far presented, this appears to be the most reasonable one.

In general it seems that most people *feel* a fate which runs through their lives and that 'there is more to all this than meets the eye'. Others perhaps convince themselves that fateful forces are an objective fact in order to retain the belief in Heaven, or some force of Universal Sentience, numinous but maddeningly invisible.

(iv) There is yet a fourth category of person with a further stance on the undecided question of a Fate/no Fate. These are the people who live sincere and meaningful lives without committing themselves to finally answering the question. Is this perhaps the wisest stance, or the most cowardly? Certainly it is a humble one before a question of such importance. Those who can thus suspend their judgment, in the face of both logic and experience, are either those with little interest in interior questions or, conversely, the seekers; those who have their mind on this and related subjects in a highly concentrated way.

Whatever the position one holds in relation to the idea of Fate (and we can hold all four at different times) the question has always been of concern to mankind for the obvious reason that we must all face death. The question itself is therefore real, personal, and always relevant. The inevitability of death makes it so.

In Taoist thought as it is to be interpreted from the *I Ching*, the questions relating to Fate become increasingly clear. According to the Principle of Opposites, the rearrangement of hexagrams I postulate is logical and accurate. Its application to

Karma is new, and more details and subtler associations will reveal themselves and bear fruit in further study. I know of no other work in which the *I Ching* is related to *real Karmic cycles*, and therefore take full responsibility for the way in which I have interpreted and presented the information in this book, and for its treatment and development of the ancient ideas to be found in the original *I Ching*.

Karma and Destiny in the I Ching

> There is in man . . . a fate that lends power to his life. And
> if he succeeds in assigning the right place to life and to
> fate, then bringing the two into harmony he puts his fate
> on a firm footing.
>
> The *I Ching*
> Wilhelm/Baynes translations.

This statement is crystal clear and many ideas immediately
spring from it regarding the position of the *I Ching* and of
Taoist thought generally on the question of Fate. The most
obvious, is that for the Taoist masters Fate is; it *exists* in the
life of an individual; physical life is 'attached' to physical death;
a natural corollary of having a physical form. The second point
is equally clear: Fate is a power or a force, 'death' as an event
evokes much greater power than the life manifested in the
physical form, and the invisible realm to which death is a door
is the source of the power of Fate.

Fate can be understood as an impulsion, an unseen shape
which defines a person's journey through life. The relationship
between a person and his Fate presents an equation which the
individual must discover if he is to come to terms with his life.
This is the curious paradox. The *I Ching* persistently suggests
that if one tries actively to oppose Fate, one will experience
misfortune. So Fate may also be conceived as 'direction',
volition, path of destiny. Where self and Fate are opposed,
unhappiness results. It seems, therefore, that Fate can be
characterised as a separate entity with which we must make our
peace if we are to live a fortunate and happy life. Yet it is
misleading to think of Fate as something which is distinct from
and outside ourselves. A person and his Fate are inextricably
entwined; Fate and the individual are part of each other. The

idea of there being any kind of separation, like a physical separation, is therefore absurd. Fate, then, can be conceived as being a part of ourselves.

In the *I Ching* there is constant use of the expressions *superior man* and *inferior man*. It is a fundamental to this work that the *superior man* refers to that part in each person which is his higher being, and the *inferior man*, to that part which is lower. When we consult it, therefore, the *I Ching* addresses the superior man, which, of its nature, controls the inferior man. The superior man is fearless. The inferior man is afraid. When we work with the *I Ching*, we seek to *resonate* with and contact the superior force, the fearless. Thus, when we consult it, we should always ask ourselves, 'What am I afraid of?' Only the inferior man will answer.

When the superior man in each of us is in control of our lives, and determines what we do and think, then, says the *I Ching*, we will have good fortune. Thus, we can say that by 'Fate', the *I Ching* means the *superior man*, that part of us which is capable of embracing good fortune, and it is to this part that we must be reconciled.

There are, however, situations in which intuition tells us that the *I Ching*'s references to superior and inferior apply not only to the inner workings of our own minds and hearts, but to those of other people as they interact with us in given circumstances (frames, or pictures of change). The second part of the *I Ching*, Hexagrams 33–64, refers to 'frames' or circumstances where this may be the case. No set of cognitive rules can delineate exactly when this distinction applies since self-awareness is largely an intuitive matter, but generally the existing division in the *I Ching* is the best guide.

We know intuitively when we have the distinction right. We are aware of ourselves as people acting either from the higher self or the lower. In many ways, one can say that the *I Ching* is an ingenious tool designed to teach that precise distinction to the individual when he turns to it for guidance, the most important distinction a person can make about himself. This is why the *I Ching* asserts that by bringing Fate and life into harmony the individual 'puts his fate on a firm footing'. He understands himself sufficiently well to act in accordance with his own higher self. We can also say that Fate, in its Taoist sense, means the ultimate reconciliation of one's lower with one's higher self. Each of the hexagrams, and each of the changes, depicts a mode or framework for this dynamic exchange, specifically in the first thirty-one hexagrams, which refer to the relationship between the inferior and superior man and to destiny.

Quite logically, then, everything we do in life is designed to effect this reconciliation. We attract events, situations and circumstances so that we may have opportunities to make this equation with Fate. When the dynamic is working correctly we also repel frames of references (combinations of people or events) preventing their reception. The dynamics of attraction and repulsion are crucial to understanding the Tao of Karma.

Only when we have completed our journey of life, or Karma, can we meet Fate. But if we *know* that this is what we are preparing to do, we can act with greater awareness in our lives, thus every situation can become a challenge designed for us by Fate. It is these circumstances, crossroads and events in our lives which are pictured in the changes (or lines). These changes can be more clearly interpreted by the individual on his journey towards his Fate through a process of distillation of opposites set in clear progressions. It is indeed beneficial to have some intimation of one's Karmic landscape.

Hitherto, there had been no recognised or established 'Tao of Karma'. The reason for this may be that the idea of Karma, as described here, is so implicit in the Taoist view that it cannot be isolated in the same way, for instance, as the concept of Reincarnation is expressed in the *Bhagavad Gita*. Yet there are interesting similarities. The dialogue between Krishna and Arjuna is a dialogue between the inferior and the superior man. Although there is a difference in presentation and language, Krishna's message is no different from the Taoists', namely that the reconciliation between higher and lower is the Karmic process which will culminate in Fate. This is also the basis of the psychology of C.J. Jung and indeed all good psychology.

The *I Ching* is not merely a system of thought or a universal philosophy: it is a mirror of the Tao itself. Presented as a mathematical symmetry, it is unique among the philosophies of the world in that it conceives of the *idea of change as a living force*. I emphasise this simply to make it clear that one cannot speak about Karma without speaking about change. That is why working with the *I Ching* compels the user to become aware of the changes within himself *as they are occurring*. That is to say, the *I Ching in its form* embodies the truth of the Tao as a reflection of the Tao, rather than merely setting it forth as if it were something static, other than itself. No other system of philosophy has this dimension, and it is the reason why this presentation of the Taoist system of Karma is so precise.

It should therefore be clear that if we consider Fate in the manner described above, and recognise Karma as our journey through life, taking this objective and mathematically precise view, then the perennial confusion between free will and Fate (or determinism) is resolved, and the parameters are defined. Our purpose in life is to meet our Fate. This is not to be equated, as it is by many, with the moment of *physical* death. Meeting our Fate in life is perceived here as a reconciliation with one's higher self and is to be experienced as death *and* re-birth. Most people have a terrible fear of death, and in these terms such fear is slavery. Karma is largely the overcoming of fear — becoming strong. Fear of death is our greatest Karmic challenge.

We have no choice in this matter of Fate. It will come. It is already determined, but if we know and accept this wholeheart-edly, our greater awareness will incorporate our free will and give us *control over the quality of our lives*. The quality of our lives can become a matter of choice, of will, of appreciating life in detail. It is in the quality of our lives that we can express our freedom. The word 'quality' here means not *what* a person does, but *how* he does it, whatever it may be.

This idea can be illustrated in a very simple metaphor. It may be our unavoidable Fate to walk along a particular road, the Karmic road. Our choice is in *how* we walk, whether positively or negatively. By opposition we can make that walk a nightmare, an agony. We can complain, drag our feet, refuse to look at the scenery, not talk to passers-by, decline offers of company, refuse to help others. We can even crawl all the way if we want. If, when finally we arrive at our journey's end we have had a terrible time and did not enjoy it at all, then we will regret ever embarking on it in the first place. We can go further still, blaming Fate and not ourselves for giving us such a terrible time.

In fact, Fate had nothing to do with it. *Fate was the destination (destiny). Karma was the journey*. How we coped with and responded to the various landmarks, i.e. situations, people, experiences (the *content* of life), depended upon our *Free Will*. We had the choice to make the best of it or not. Only we could spoil the journey. This principle can be stated and restated in innumerable different ways, but the distinction is vital. *We choose*. We are responsible for the quality of our lives, and because everything is interconnected, *we choose* and are therefore also responsible for the quality of everybody else's life. Thus our individual choice has universal consequences.

The central purpose of this book is to make the point that if we know we are going to meet our Fate, and our journey towards it is Karma, we can be conscious of our lives and take responsibility for enriching them to our fullest capability. Yet, because everything is interconnected, we can only realise our full positive energy potential if everybody else does so as well. We are thereby inhibited and diminished to the extent that others do not make this attempt.

In *The I Ching on Love* (Blandford Press, 1984), I underlined that the purpose and function of the *I Ching* is to act as an evolutionary tool so that those seeking guidance and personal orientation among its changes can learn to make the most of their abilities, fulfil their potential. In the context of understanding the Taoist view of Karma and Destiny, that purpose remains the same. In this book, therefore, I have tried to help the reader to recognise his Karmic landscape, and if only one person has been enabled to crash through that brick wall which is common to us all or to leap the abyss, it will have been worthwhile. One hopes that successful comprehension will be global, however.

In Waley's translation of the *Tao Te Ching** we read these remarkable words of Lao Tsu:

Push far enough toward the Void,
Hold fast enough to Quietness,
And of the ten thousand things, none but can be worked on
　by you.

---

*The Wildwood House edition of *Tao Te Ching* is also strongly recommended.

I have beheld them, whither they go back.
See, all things howsoever they flourish
Return to the root from which they grew.
This return to the root is called Quietness;
Quietness is called the submission to Fate;
What has submitted to Fate has become part of the
        always-so*.
To know the always-so is to be illumined;
Not to know it, means to go blindly to disaster.

He who knows the always-so has room in him for
        everything;
He who has room in him for everything is without
        prejudice.
To be without prejudice is to be kingly;
To be kingly is to be of heaven;
To be of heaven is to be in Tao.
Tao is forever and he that possesses it,
Though his body ceases, is not destroyed.

---

*The expression *the always-so* is usually rendered, more poetically, as *the Eternal*, or *Eternity – The Forever Present*. Wittgenstein in his Tractatus said: 'If we take eternity not to mean infinite temporal duration, then eternal life exists for those who live in the present.' He was therefore saying exactly the same thing as Lao Tsu, that *eternity is a state of mind*. In the light of this truth death becomes brilliant, means Completion – Illumination.

Death, Rebirth
and Reincarnation

It seems perfectly natural to think of our lives as being a continuum with two measurable, finite ends. We live our allotted time, 'and then are heard no more'. The great questions arising from this view, that we come into this world once and leave it forever, are often ignored by western philosophers, although they form the basis of the Christian belief. In the East, however, among Buddhists and Hindus, it is traditional to think of death in a different way. They believe that a man's soul reincarnates; returns again and again, taking up different bodies and the lives related to them, until he becomes Unified, one with Brahman (God), or the Enlightened One, and then he need return no more. This idea of reincarnation has begun to find its way increasingly into western thought and literature, in some circles, in the last half of this century.

Our fear of death fuels our fascination for the many concepts which point towards immortality. The Pharaohs, for instance, were so preoccupied with it that they built vast monuments and designed great ceremonies to ease their passage from life to life. Yet many people find no discomfort in contemplating this life as their only one which, when it is over, leaves nothing behind, neither memory nor trace. No meeting with loved ones in some heavenly existence beyond the grave. Others find such nothing-ness terrifying, making a mockery of our lives, lending neither significance, rhyme nor reason to our actions during our time upon this earth.

How then should one think of 'continuance' or 'lack of continuance' – as beings, or forces of sentience, or points of consciousness? It is a profound, unresolved cosmological problem which has beguiled poets and writers through the ages. Rilke captures the essence of it in his wonderful poem the *Ninth Elegy* where he writes:

16

Not because happiness really exists, that precipitate
profit of imminent loss.
Not out of curiosity, not just to practice the heart,
that could still be there in laurel . . .
But because being here is much, and because all this
that's here, so fleeting, seems to require us and strangely
concerns us. Us the most fleeting of all. Just once,
everything, only for once. Once and no more. And we,
too,
once. And never again. But this
having been once on earth – can it ever be cancelled?

How eloquently Rilke distils these thoughts which have
passed through most people's minds, in some form or another,
at some stage in their lives. The awareness of this numinous
dimension has caused men and women to rouse themselves to
great deeds. Yet, despite great deeds, destiny or fate, the
question persists without any new certainty to assuage our
thirst for the waters of eternal life. The ideas are there. Every
religion promises it, no doubt because it is true, and the
common conception of life as a finite, beginning and ending
affair of the body, is in fact a misconception. Despite the rule of
reason in the West, deep in our hearts these great questions
attract us not only because we fear death, but because we intuit
or 'know' that in a cosmic sense we do not 'end' or die. We
know there is more to us than the passing life of our bodies and
we feel profoundly, inexpressibly, sure that we are already
immortal – that we have an immortal soul, for: 'even the
noticing beasts are aware that we don't feel very securely at
home in this interpreted world', says Rilke in *The First Elegy*.

So, the search goes on – for something we have never lost.
Therefore, when we speak of Karma, we are talking of the
journey of our souls. Karma is the road our spirit travels on its
journey towards Illumination, Fate, the Centre of the Wheel,
Heaven, whatever we may call it. And if this is the truth then
death, as Milton proclaims in *Paradise Lost*, is no death at all.
'By the fruit, it gives thee life to Knowledge.'

The idea of reincarnation, therefore, confirms that when we
die we are reborn continuously through time in a cyclic motion,
each death a transcendence, spiralling our souls towards higher

Fates, until we are at one with the Highest Self at the heart of the Universe. Ultimately, though 'still dressed in flesh', we may transcend that numinous veil which seers and conscious men have shown us to be a living experience, and emerge perfected beings. The *I Ching* speaks of these mysteries which increasingly become certainties with every turn of the spiral of conscious evolution: 'All that is visible must grow beyond itself and extend into the realm of the invisible. Thereby it receives its true consecration and clarity and takes root in the cosmic order.'

In Mahayana Buddhism it is said that the Aspirant deliberately delays his emergence into full Buddhahood in order to help others reach perfection also. His work, therefore, is not in one life, but in a huge dimension of time, 'A whole rosary of lives threaded upon one personality', as Sir Arthur Conan Doyle so beautifully expressed it. Finally, having completed his task, the Aspirant achieves the full glory of Buddhahood. From the beginning this becomes the whole purpose of his existence; everything he does life after life is towards that single aim. It is in this spirit that the great Lotus Sutra is to be understood:

> The dull, who delight in petty rules,
> Who are greedily attached to mortality,
> Who have not, under countless Buddhas,
> Walked the profound and mystic way,
> Who are harassed by all the suffering –
> To these I preach Nirvana.
> Such is the expedient I employ
> To lead them to Buddha – Wisdom.
>
> Not yet could I say to them
> 'You shall all attain to Buddhahood',
> For the time had not yet arrived.
> *But Now the Very Time Has Come*
> And I must preach the Great Vehicle . . .
> My final seal of the Law . . . is now Announced.

Here, as in the *I Ching*, and in all the world's great religious texts, the transcendental state of being is manifested in those who help raise mankind to a higher plateau of spiritual reality. It is therefore as much a fact for the times we live in, as it is a

Universal for all time: 'That every event in the visible world is the effect of an image, that is, of an idea, in the unseen world.' This is expressed succinctly in the Hermetic doctrine by the well-known phrase: 'as above, so below'.

Karmic Numbers

THE MACRO-CYCLE

The expressions 'Macro' and 'Micro' cycles are, of course, relative. 'Macro' can represent the span of one's whole life, or something much longer, i.e. a millennium. 'Micro' may refer to one day in a lifetime, or one second in a day. In this book, however, the term 'Macro-cycle' refers to the six Karmic progressions already described, and to those junctures, situations, moments of change, which occur *and* recur – *not necessarily in chronological time* – in the span of a person's life. Thus, when following the descriptions of the Karmic pictures of change in the appropriate sections of this book, the reader will recognise those situations which, like blueprints, characterise the various *frames* with which they intersect the whole Karma and Destiny 'reality grid' as here interpreted.

THE MICRO-CYCLE

While the six Karmic steps, germane to each individual life, represent the Macro (or larger) cycle, the reader needs to understand that the system presented is complete and dynamic. Thus, an individual does not go backwards and forwards only through his six steps as projected here, although these are the six principal ones, and conceal the main challenge. In reality, in daily life each individual is engaged in a parallel 'Micro-cycle', and will pass through each and every one of the situations presented throughout this book at some time or another in their life, some situations occurring more frequently than others. We all experience these stages to a greater or lesser extent, depending on the disposition of our personality and character.

All the Karmic numbers and progressions refer to our main challenges, and have been arranged as *frames of action*, intending to embrace the principal dynamics of an individual's life. As long as we live, we will meet with these challenges. These frames (or pictures) refer to the relationship between the superior and inferior elements in our specific nature. Each step is as much a reference point in relation to the *whole person* as it is in the universal context. Understood as a map, the steps (or frames) are the main (macro) identifying points of intersection by which our inner and outer worlds may be orientated. At any point in one's life one or more of these frames can act as a meaningful and relevant signpost. These are compass points of a spiritual nature, which have their correspondence in the world of action. Thus, they are therefore recognisable as frames of action, containing descriptions of the ambience, or mood, in which the action may take place.

KARMIC ROOTS

The validity of this system requires no belief. It stands on its own and carries its own proofs within its structure. Comprehension comes with use. It is important, therefore, that the section on the Karmic root number signified by the hexagram which forms the basis of the whole progression, should be read with care. Broader association will bear fruit for the attentive reader, towards unfolding for each person that enhanced quality of life which the *I Ching* calls *The Superior Way*.

THE KARMIC NUMBER

The western calendar was originally based on the cycles of the moon and does not conflict with the ancient Chinese calendar. Thus the number of the day of one's birth, without regard to month or year, is the significant point in this system. As we are dealing with the Macro-cycle only, this information is sufficient, and the book is divided, therefore, into thirty-one sections beginning with the first day of the month.

All the reader needs to do is look up his birthday. It does not matter whether it is the 11th of April or the 11th of September: the Karmic number is eleven. Under the relevant day a summary of the Karmic root hexagram will be found from which the Karmic steps are derived. This describes the psychological atmosphere of the whole journey, and is followed by a description of the six Karmic steps which indicate the challenges each will meet and the conflicting relationship between the superior and inferior in each individual. Each reader will be able to determine for himself on which level the personal information applies according to his degree of self-knowledge, which will deepen with the careful use of this system.

The System

THE PRINCIPLE OF OPPOSITES

The Principle of Opposites postulates that everything eventually transforms itself into its opposite state. The whole construction of the concept of Karma in the *I Ching* is founded on this simple dynamic; from it all the changes are derived. For the sake of clarity the following example is given.

The *I Ching* is composed of sixty-four sections – or pictures of change – and each section is called a hexagram. A hexagram is a picture of six-dimensional change which in the *I Ching* is represented by six lines of equal length placed one on top of the other (and always counted from the bottom). Each of the six lines which comprise a hexagram refers to six smaller pictures of change within any one hexagram or big picture of change. These are called 'the lines' or, more appropriately, 'the changes'. It is this idea of progressive or evolutionary change which makes the *I Ching* and its sixty-four hexagrams unique. Their arrangement is exact and together they form a picture of reality, or, as it is traditionally known, Tao. What is remarkable in the *I Ching*'s representation of Tao is its insistence that no picture of reality is complete unless it includes the idea of change. It is in this assertion that a great deal of western philosophy flounders. Thus, while the arrangement of the *I Ching* is 'a picture of the dynamics of reality', it is only a picture and nothing more. It cannot represent the true Tao, as the true Tao changes. The actual arrangement, then, is a *quiescent* or passive representation – until it is activated by use. Only then does it transform miraculously into the true state of Tao, for while the *I Ching* is one pole, inactive and static, we individuals are the other, dynamic and charged. When we connect, like an electrical circuit, at the opposite end, the whole structure comes alive and ceases to be quiescent; it becomes a dynamic mirror reflecting the changes within us. The implications of this reflection are far-reaching, but for the purpose of this book, it is necessary to show how the *I Ching*'s specific arrangement of pictures can be reorganised in order to give us the steps to be climbed if we are to interact with our Karma. A clue may be found in the words.of hexagram 1: The Creative, '. . . he sees with great clarity causes and effects, he completes the six steps at the right time and mounts toward heaven on them at the right time as though on six dragons.'

The Taoist Principle of Karma defines and *focuses* upon those six steps, thus 'revealing to man his destiny, and the design of his Fate' which is the essential purpose of the *I Ching*. The basic principle works like this:

Example: Hexagram 24: RETURN (The Turning Point)

The direction of progressions (or *Karmic steps*) is upward from line 1 through to 6

If all the lines in the above hexagram changed simultaneously, it would transform into exactly the opposite hexagram. All the broken lines would become unbroken or yang lines; and the single (unbroken) or yang line would become broken or yin lines. It would therefore appear like this:

All the lines have reversed. This hexagram is the inverse of 24.

44

This hexagram is called *Coming to Meet (Meeting Point)*, *number 44*. For those who are unfamiliar with the *I Ching*, the circle in line one of hexagram 24 of the example is a symbol used to denote in a yang or unbroken line that it is *about to change in to its opposite*; the crosses likewise are symbols used for yin, or broken, lines indicating where they will become their opposite – yang lines.

It is also to be observed that the changes represented by the lines in the hexagrams always change *in parallel*. Therefore, in hexagram 24 line one, a yang, or unbroken, line is about to change *to the corresponding position in hexagram 44*, in other words, to the position of line one in hexagram 44 – a yin line. This is so for all the other lines. Ingenious stuff!

The example above shows what results when all the lines in a hexagram change *at once*. Here, however, we are concerned with the lines changing *one by one*. When this happens, instead of generating the opposite hexagram, it generates a series of six hexagrams which give rise to the six steps, ending in the exact opposite of the original hexagram. It works very simply, as follows. Using the hexagrams above we can discover the six Karmic progressions for the Karmic number 24:

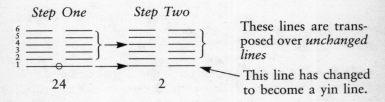

Step One   *Step Two*

These lines are transposed over *unchanged lines*

This line has changed to become a yin line.

24   2

One moving line transforms the whole into a new hexagram. Chess is the perfect analogy for this idea.

It is obvious here that only line one, the yang line, is moving towards its opposite; all the other lines in hexagram 24 remain the same, and are transposed into the new hexagram created by the single moving line, unchanged. It only takes one moving line in a hexagram, in any position, to generate a totally new picture of change.

Thus, in this example, line one moves, the others do not, and hexagram 2: The Receptive is created. Now, this is very important if the scheme of Karmic progressions is to be made clear: the line which has become its opposite is now, in the example, *line one of hexagram 2. It is this line which is resonating*, creating the new picture from the transformation of the old (line one in hexagram 24). It is this new picture we have now to look at.

We take the new hexagram, now hexagram 2: The Receptive:

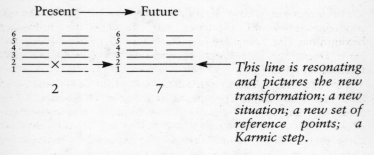

Present ——————► Future

2   7

This line is resonating and pictures the new transformation; a new situation; a new set of reference points; a Karmic step.

Notes: lines 1, 3, 4, 5 and 6 remain unchanged

As we are engaged in working step by step through a Karmic progression (in this example) from hexagram 24 to its opposite, 44, the steps, 1, 2, 3, 4, 5, 6, appear and are depicted like a ladder, progressing in sequence from the bottom. Line one of hexagram 24 has changed to produce hexagram 2: The Receptive. Line *two* of hexagram 2 now moves in order to generate a new hexagram, in this case, hexagram 7: The Army (Challenge).

This same principle of line by line transformation is carried through in exactly the same way until all the six steps are established in their corresponding positions, and the cycle of Karma is complete (or more precisely the *picture* of the cycle of Karma is complete). Thus the Macro-cycle for *Karmic number 24* looks like this:

Hexagram 24 Hexagram 2   Hexagram 7   Hexagram 46 Hexagram 32 Hexagram 28

And finally as illustrated above:

Hexagram 44

For a person whose Karmic number is 24, their Karmic progressions would therefore run through the following hexagrams: The Receptive (2); The Army (7); Pushing Upward (46); Duration (32); Preponderance of the Great (28); and Coming to Meet (44).

This process applies to each of the sixty-four hexagrams, and their individual Karmic progressions are given in this book. The result is, that *all the changes* cross-connect in a pattern of possibilities or circumstances, and relate to the individual as their pictures of Karmic change. Applying the Principle of Opposites we are able to derive mathematical pathways and precise correspondences which have significance and meaning for each individual in the real world, i.e. in action.

The basic essential dynamics of Karma and Destiny in the *I Ching* have been explained above and the reader does not need to work the progressions out for himself. What is of importance is that the individual climbs six steps. The seventh is Heaven.

The six steps

The following six steps picture the principal stages through which the life will pass, and each represents one or all of the following:

      (i) a major challenge
     (ii) a major change
    (iii) a major point of personal evolution

Through these six steps each individual may attain self-realisation, completion, enlightenment. They represent precisely the Karma of the individual's life, through which clusters of personal relationships and events may come to have meaning. It is important to realise that these six steps do not necessarily occur in chronological order in any individual's life, but invariably manifest themselves in different combinations, usually recognisable by familiar feelings, circumstances or situations.

PART TWO

The Karmic Progressions

The Macro-Cycle

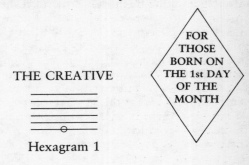

THE CREATIVE

Hexagram 1

FOR
THOSE
BORN ON
THE 1st DAY
OF THE
MONTH

> *Your Karmic number is 1 (Heaven-oriented). One is the number of the creative principle. It is also the number of natural strength. This will manifest itself as independence, wilfulness, a balance of logic and intuition and a pronounced aptitude for leadership and the taking of initiative. These qualities misused can make you appear cold, Machiavellian and insensitive. You have the ability to make risks pay off – take risks.*

YOUR ROOT HEXAGRAM: HEXAGRAM 1

Your root hexagram gives the climate or ambience of the six Karmic pictures which are the principal characteristics of your Karmic journey.

The main characteristics of 'The Creative' are the regeneration of energy, the conception of ideas, the unity of matter and spirit, and the ability to initiate action. Responsibility, leadership, and a sense of vocation are implicit in 'The Creative'. In Taoist terms, this hexagram represents the source of all that exists and all that may exist in the future, therefore it harbours within it the idea of what is to come, the idea of potential.

For people with a Karmic number of 1, there will be an

31

emphasis throughout their lives on growth, spiritual as well as emotional. You will be very keenly aware of the evolution of your consciousness through your experiences. You will have no trouble intuiting the higher order of reality as it manifests itself on earth. However you contact your higher self, inspiration will never truly desert you. You will always feel a drive to better yourself, and you will feel a need to be constantly active. You view all your hopes, ambitions and desires as part of a greater scheme of self-improvement, and this infuses your life with a sense of purpose and determination which you do not have to cultivate as it is part of the way you are.

'Heaven oriented' means you look upwards, and in another sense, you are able to view the world from an elevated point of perception, as if looking downward from heaven.

Step One: Hexagram 44 (Meeting and Compromise)

If you experience drawbacks in the course of your life, especially during times when you are engaged in activities which will advance your position in the world, or at times when you are about to undergo transitions or transformations, it will be due to bad influences. Such influence will have at its source either those people in your past who do not mean well by you and so 'plot' and 'intrigue' against you or bad habits or traits in your own character which you have not consciously eradicated.

In the transition from inferior to superior, this kind of influence can constantly rear its head at the critical moment and so impede your progress. The most important point is that you are stronger than the bad influence, and thus able to neutralise its effect.

Step Two: Hexagram 33 (Strategic Withdrawal)

You are going to find yourself in some pretty tight spots, but you will escape by the skin of your teeth every time, not due to your own courage, foresight and resourcefulness, but due to the courage, foresight and resourcefulness of someone looking out for you.

The superior man rescues the inferior man in his moment of desperation. The inferior man never forgets the experience. The inferior man learns to be prepared. The superior man forgives.

Step Three: Hexagram 12 (Superficiality/Standstill)

You are tempted to travel a false road. The road bears the characteristics of great challenges and obstacles which are far beyond your ability to cope with. The falsity lies in your own ego, in your assumption that you are more able than you really are. This is the inferior man. The superior man realises the plight of the inferior man and forces him to turn back and take stock of himself and thereby they are reconciled in choosing the correct road. This is represented as a course of action to which you are equal.

Step Four: Hexagram 20 (A View of the World)

The superior man is a man of ability who is able to perceive the needs of the people and his relative usefulness to them. The inferior man must not exploit the superior man's dedication to service. This pictures a situation where the superior man must be honoured and given sufficient freedom to act without constraining supervision, as this is an insult to a man of ability. The superior man must be properly rewarded, the inferior man must desist from selfishness and bigotry.

Step Five: Hexagram 23 (Separation)

When the inferior man grows close to the superior man, the superior man's influence is stronger. Thus it is the inferior man that is increased rather than the superior man decreased.

Each person has good and bad qualities. Sometimes the bad elements of a person's character get the better of the good elements. Here the dynamic pictures that conflict are a recurring cycle, but good always gets the better of bad. Darkness cannot flourish in the light.

Step Six: Hexagram 2 (The Receptive)

Since you were born under the Karmic number 1, opposite forces are felt very keenly. The good is very good, the bad is very bad. The light is very bright, the dark is very dark. In Step Five, the light wins without experiencing any harm to itself and without entering into any direct conflict, for in that situation, the inferior man approached the superior man, but was immediately overcome by the natural force of the superior man.

Here, however, the inferior man is stronger, as strong as the superior man. Thus there is a battle between them. This is the fight for self-control, self-discipline. The superior man is destined to win, but not without a substantial drain of energy which will require him to recuperate afterwards.

Synthesis

People born under Karmic number 1 have an even mix of weakness and strength. Weakness undermines strength, thus making you less effective. Strength overcomes weakness, thus making you more effective.

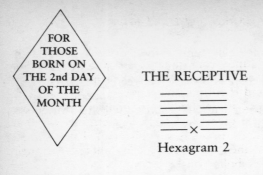

FOR
THOSE
BORN ON
THE 2nd DAY
OF THE
MONTH

THE RECEPTIVE

Hexagram 2

Your Karmic number is 2 (Earth-oriented). You were born with a natural ability to handle people, but you have to believe in yourself. You have a naturally strong personality, though you can be moody. Environment is critically important to you and you should cultivate your aesthetic appreciation to the highest possible level. You have a keen sense of justice and you always try to do right by other people. Express this in worldly terms as well as on a personal level. Above all, be fair to yourself.

YOUR ROOT HEXAGRAM: HEXAGRAM 2

Your root hexagram gives the climate or ambience of the six Karmic pictures which are the principal characteristics of your Karmic journey.

The main characteristics of 'The Receptive' are quietness, warmth, an all-embracing kindness. It is the pure symbol of the earth. Without the receptive principle, the creative principle cannot manifest itself in the real world and thus it is true to say that 'The Receptive' is the manifestation in every sense of the creative principle and its form is the earth.

People whose Karmic root number is 2 are capable of a universality and the embracing of all the nurturing and growth dynamics which are associated with the earth. This includes the idea of physical, spiritual and mental fertility. These people have a natural understanding of the spirit that moves things. This understanding is so innate that they do not have to think about it.

In Taoist terms, like the number 1, number 2 is the only other pure number, and from numbers 1 and 2 all other numbers can be derived. This is why they are symbolised in the *I Ching* as Heaven and Earth incarnate.

In personal terms, 2 is the number of rejuvenation. These people are able to keep themselves fresh in the same way that all the seasons have a freshness about them. They are all distinct, all new in their own way, even though in their interrelations they symbolise birth, bloom, decay and death. Thus this Karmic root lends to those born under it the ability to divide and make whole. This could manifest itself, among other ways, as the ability to organise and to perceive diversity in unity and unity in diversity.

The essence of 2 is that it gives 1 the dimension of reality. In physical terms, this characterises the dimension of space, and therefore form. Form cannot exist except in space. But the essence of all form is 1. This is what is meant when it is said that numbers 1 and 2 are complementary and together form reality.

It should therefore be obvious why 2 is earth-oriented – in itself it is a pure symbol of earth in so far as it is the manifestation of the Creative in its pure, primordial form.

Step One: Hexagram 24 (The Moment of Transition)

The superior man has an instinct for well-timed and appropriate action. In the development of character, this is a recurring motif. The inferior man is tempted to digress and overlook obvious potholes in the road ahead. The inferior man does not look where he is going and so walks into difficulties that could easily have been avoided. The superior man plans routes around difficulties before they are encountered.

Step Two: Hexagram 19 (The Open Door)

The superior man takes a wider, more philosophical view of life than the inferior man. This pictures one who clearly perceives his fate, recognises the inevitability of death, and so the fleetingness of life, and this perspective lends a superior power of volition to the actions of the superior man. The picture is of one who, even in adversity, is able to feel positive. This is superior wisdom at its best.

Step Three: Hexagram 11 (Peace)

The picture here is a variation on the earlier picture. The inferior man is easily influenced by misfortune and becomes selfish and narrow-minded as a result of it, thereby giving way to chaotic influences which are the essence of the inferior man. The superior man understands that good and bad fortune can sometimes be the product of outside events which nevertheless, and through no fault of his own, affect him – like a ship caught in an unforecast squall. The superior man knows that any deviation from his immediate course is not a deviation from his Karmic journey towards Fate, and therefore in the true sense is able to steer a steady course all the way through. The inferior man does not know this and therefore suffers.

Your superiority lies and is tested in your ability to act with quality in times of adversity. You know that acting with quality in such times is a matter of choice which is, when properly understood, no choice at all for the superior man.

Step Four: Hexagram 34 (The Leading Initiative)

The Karmic picture realises a position of dominance for the superior man. You are the leader, quietly making progress without conflict or intimidation from the inferior man. The Karmic road is clear. This is a period of plain sailing, one of many such in your life. This is a fortunate Karmic trait.

Step Five: Hexagram 43 (Personal Resolution)

The inferior man directly opposes the superior man. The inferior is strong and tries to force the superior man to abandon the battle. He is tempted to do so for fear of losing. The realisation that abandoning the battle is losing to the inferior man is a superior realisation, and it is this which causes the superior to stand up to the inferior.

The Karmic picture is that of standing your ground when it is right to do so. The inferior man is tempting you to step off *your* path and go around him, but there is no way round him. Stand your ground. What effect does this have on the inferior man?

Step Six: Hexagram 1 (The Creative)

The picture is one of the inferior man looking back over the successes and achievements of the superior man and thinking them his own. The inferior man is walking down the Karmic road looking over his shoulder. He does not see the holes in the road. The superior man keeps his eyes on the road and is not concerned with the vainglory that is important to the inferior man.

The picture is one of subtle self-deception which must be resisted when it is most greatly attracted: after achievement.

Synthesis

Karmic number 2 is one of the most fortunte roads to Fate. There are many clear patches for achievement. Don't let it go to your head. For the superior man, vainglory tends to be neutralised by a sense of humour.

DIFFICULT BEGINNINGS

FOR
THOSE
BORN ON
THE 3rd DAY
OF THE
MONTH

Hexagram 3

> *Your Karmic number is 3 (Heaven-oriented). You are creative and talented and sociable. You must choose fields of activity which enable you to fulfil the promise of your imagination, which is especially well endowed. Do not give in to superficiality, though this will become less of a temptation as your creative abilities mature through expression.*

YOUR ROOT HEXAGRAM: HEXAGRAM 3

Your root hexagram gives the climate or ambience of the six Karmic pictures which are the principal characteristics of your Karmic journey.

Three is the number of unity. It is the natural offspring of 1 and 2, the Creative and Receptive principles. It is at once the symbol of synthesis, birth, and new beginnings. It is therefore the number of potential, hope, possibility, and represents the first node of growth. Three has within it the capacity for perfection. Inherent in its nature are the seeds of 1 and 2 from which it arose, therefore it is also the symbol of perfection. The implication for mankind is that he has already within him the capacity for spiritual perfection.

Three symbolises the first step in the proof of an evolutionary process of perfection, but because everything is still to come, it is called 'Difficulty at the Beginning'. Thus for the number 3 person, the early part of life as a whole will be a struggle, and anyone who has this hexagram figured in their Karmic progression will experience the characteristics of number 3 as it manifests itself in the formulation of their ideas and projects.

As the pure number of synthesis, hexagram 3 is also the pure symbol of inspiration.

Step One: Hexagram 8 (The Leading Initiative)

The inferior man and the superior man are on frank speaking terms. The result is that what tends to be expressed in your work and your dealings with others is heartfelt and true. This is a picture of honesty.

Step Two: Hexagram 29 (The Twilight of the Spirit)

The inferior man is keen, eager, ambitious and full of self-confidence. In itself, this is harmless. In relation to the superior man, who regulates the energy, informs the direction and guides the inferior man, there is the possibility of steady achievement.

The picture is of a highly energetic inferior man. For this energy to come to something, the superior man must be correspondingly strong. Again, inferior and superior elements are on speaking terms. Thus there is every possibility of co-operation and self-control.

Step Three: Hexagram 48 (The Well)

This pictures a superior man who is isolated. He works on with great ability, but without the notice of others. The inferior man is frustrated, but his frustration does not impede the work of the superior man, nor does it bring the superior man to the attention of others. It is better for the inferior man to go to sleep and let the superior man work.

Step Four: Hexagram 28 (Under Pressure)

The superior man is friendly and this makes other superior men regard him with trust. The inferior man is tempted to take advantage of the superior man's position of confidence in order to protect himself. If he does so, the superior man will be harmed. The superior man does not misuse advantage to conceal his thoughts.

Step Five: Hexagram 32 (Durability)

You are confronted by a fork in the road. The inferior man wants to take one path, the superior man the other. The superior man is single-minded, but is aware of the alternatives.

The inferior man is narrow-minded and is not aware of the superior man. The superior man must decide the path. This is an exercise of willpower.

Step Six: Hexagram 50 (The Cauldron/Valuable Work)

This pictures a dialogue between the superior man and the inferior man. The inferior man asks the superior man for advice in order to reconcile himself to the ways of the superior man. The superior man gives the advice. His superiority in giving the advice extends beyond the subject of the advice itself to the way in which it is given. The superior man gives advice in a gentle, but firm way, and in a perfectly good spirit of kindness. The inferior man takes the advice of the superior man.

Synthesis

In general terms, the relationship between the inferior man and the superior man on this Karmic road is largely friendly, open and energetic. Like the relationship between father and son, here the father is wise and kind and the son is receptive and intelligent. Much fruit can grow from a relationship of this kind.

The occasional hiccup in the Karmic progression occurs when there is a battle of wills, and in this case the inferior defers to the superior more often than not.

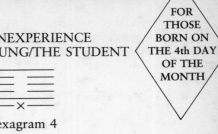

THE INEXPERIENCE
OF THE YOUNG/THE STUDENT

FOR
THOSE
BORN ON
THE 4th DAY
OF THE
MONTH

Hexagram 4

> *Your Karmic number is 4 (Earth-oriented). You are solid,
> methodical, practical and honest. Self-control is natural to
> you. Avoid a tendency to be over-materialistic, bigoted
> and giving the appearance of being a cold fish. Overcome
> your fear of showing your emotions. You like to organise
> other people, and you can be successful in this in the
> commercial world.*

YOUR ROOT HEXAGRAM: HEXAGRAM 4

Your root hexagram gives the climate or ambience of the six
Karmic pictures which are the principal characteristics of your
Karmic journey.

This is the number of early youth. It is the solid establish-
ment of the evolutionary process. It symbolises the beginnings
of awareness. The characteristic is of an individual who is
beginning to find his feet. If you have this Karmic root, you
always start at the bottom, you ask the first questions; you
break new ground; you discover new territories; you are
searching for new possibilities. You learn from your mistakes.
In the early days you need guidance because of your
unfamiliarity with the terrain, or you could harm yourself. Out
of these first experiences grow wisdom and judgment. This is
the Karmic number of the eternal student – you are always
entering upon new paths of discovery and because you are
open-minded, everything is possible.

Throughout your life, you should always have reference to
your guiding principle. This could take the form of a book of

wisdom to which you may refer whenever you enter upon a new situation, or the memory of a clear example. Choose your teachers well and they will serve you throughout your life.

Step One: Hexagram 41 (External Poverty)

The superior man is friendly and well disposed towards the inferior man, so he offers to help him. The inferior man recognises this and allows himself to be helped. However, in these circumstances, the superior man's help is not unlimited. Thus the inferior man should not allow the superior man to give everything he has as this would harm him. Thus the inferior man must himself be superior in not taking everything that is offered, but only what he needs. This is a picture of true civility.

Step Two: Hexagram 27 (Health (Body and Mind))

The situation pictured is of an inferior man who has the strength to keep pace with the demands of the superior man and the superior man's environment. Why does he not then do this? Because he is slightly overawed by the superior man and is therefore afraid. The inferior man must overcome his fear to stand on his own two feet and do more than gesture to the superior man that he is willing to do so.

Step Three: Hexagram 22 (Grace (Art and Aesthetics))

The superior man is able to partake of and enjoy to the full the transient pleasures that life may offer and which are, no doubt, deserved, without losing his perspective. The inferior man indulges in these pleasures, even to excess, and so loses perspective and his happiness.

The superior man knows how to enjoy himself without harming himself. The inferior man does not.

Step Four: Hexagram 30 (Fires of the Heart (The Clinging))

The superior man makes the resources of his personal energy last in a measured and orderly way throughout the duration of his Karmic journey. Thus he uses his talents and his energies, however great or small, in proportion to the demands of his life. The superior man has an instinct, then, for appropriate energy or appropriate force to be used in any given situation. The inferior man has no such instinct. He takes his entire life store of fire wood and starts one huge bonfire which burns extremely brightly and is visible from a long way off, but soon burns out, and in this way he uses up all his resources before their time.

Step Five: Hexagram 13 (Peace (In the World))

The most desirable relationship for the inferior man and the superior man is peaceful coexistence, with the superior man in control and as the guiding force in all events. The situation presented here is one in which the inferior and superior are so placed in relation to each other in the direst conflict (like an East-West nuclear exchange) that if they were actually to engage in battle, neither side would survive it. This is an internecine situation. The adversaries face each other with equal strength. Neither side can defend itself from the attack of the other. If either side were to attack, both would be destroyed immediately.

Thus we have the picture of maximum conflict; but here, as in the outside world, the inferior and the superior are elements of one and the same entity. Because the strength of the inferior is equal to that of the superior, the situation cannot endure in actual conflict. The natural progression of time must eventually tip the balance of power in favour of the inferior or the superior element, as they cannot be held naturally in equilibrium for very long. This is the nature of maximum tension. One side must give way to the other as a part of the natural cycle of life.

However, this situation, which must be conceived as a whole, now yields an insight to both sides, superior and inferior. The superior knows that if the inferior attacks they will both be destroyed. He has the true perspective of their relationship. The inferior does not have this. The situation can advance peaceably if the superior man can communicate to the inferior man that any attack will also destroy him. This dynamic is meant to be understood as an internal struggle. The outward manifestation of this internal struggle (reality) is reflected to the exact same degree in the outside world. The reconciliation of the inferior man with the superior man or the inferior way with the superior way (alignment with the Tao) is the central story of mankind today.

It seems worth noting that although the relative positions of inferior and superior reflect a natural and changing order which we cannot avoid, knowledge of this natural dynamic will enable us to recognise the position as and when it arises in future ages, so that the inevitability of mutual destruction arising from a conflict of these equal and opposite forces can be fully contained and understood, and therefore transcended. It is this transcendence or recognition of the Tao as it is reflected in points of equal and opposite tension that is the serious challenge to the communicative power of the superior man. Therefore, as an internal dialogue it is the power of the superior man to communicate the situation in the correct way to the inferior man which will enable the spiritual transcendence (higher comprehension) to take place in a natural way. As this takes place in the human heart, so it will take place among governments.

Step Six: Hexagram 49 (Dynamism)

There are times when the influence of the superior man over the inferior man requires radical and dynamic change in the whole spectrum of relationships between the two of them. But these changes may be dependent on the alteration of the fundamental assumptions in the relationship, that is to say, the need to rack up the whole relationship to a higher gear. The shared assumption between the inferior and the superior will now be higher than it was before. This has an effect on the potential of the relationship in its highest manifestations. The creative propensities of the individual (or the world) are vastly expanded. But the superior man is only concerned with the revolution as it affects the fundaments of his relationship with the inferior man. He is not concerned with the pedantic reform of every minuscule detail of behaviour as he knows that the reform of values in the roots of the relationship will give rise to a reformed expression of those new values in their higher levels.

The superior man understands the mechanics of evolution which is why he concentrates on changing the fundamental assumptions of relationships rather than their flowers.

Synthesis

This is a troublesome Karmic number, for the difficulties of character can have significantly bad consequences far beyond your own immediate circle of influence. You have to look at the effects of your selfishness, especially in the way your tendency to political naïvety compounds complex issues. You like to hide in that complexity and foolishly, more often than not, fall foul of it. The Karmic test is to seek simplicity in life. The more simple your view the more likely it is to be a guiding force in life. Do not think that the complex and the sophisticated (snobbish) have any real depth or meaning. It is usally a bad sign.

You also have a tendency to expect more from others than you have a right to ask, and you do not recognise the impact of such impositions. Your tendency is to overestimate and to underestimate. You find it difficult to see the actual middle way, the point of balance. Playing Devil's Advocate (usually as a form of emotional self-defence) earns you people's distrust more than it raises a smile. You also resent the impositions of others – yet you crave their company on impossible terms.

Finally, you may find yourself in a career predicament (for you are recognisably shrewd and able) where your organisational ability and, in well-balanced cases, leadership quality, are used in the service of destructive influences. You have to watch for this, as the allurements and temptations are very strong – especially for someone who thinks quite a lot of himself – and you will always end up paying for it one way or another.

In essence, you have a blind spot for the real hypocrisy because you compromise with it and then justify your position (and then you are ensnared). If you are not a student of a spiritual school you should seriously consider the option. You don't know enough about reality to keep up the pretence for a life time.

FOR
THOSE
BORN ON
THE 5th DAY
OF THE
MONTH

PATIENCE

Hexagram 5

Your Karmic number is 5 (Heaven-oriented). You are energetic and lively, enthusiastic and changeful, even dilettantish. You must have variety, and you thrive best in fast social situations. Mostly good humoured, often superficial, you must learn to concentrate, otherwise life will run fast, but not very deep.

YOUR ROOT HEXAGRAM: HEXAGRAM 5

Your root hexagram gives the climate or ambience of the six Karmic pictures which are the principal characteristics of your Karmic journey.

On the spiral of spiritual evolution, 5 is the symbol of the beginnings of initiative, informed creativity, informed discovery, the beginnings of self-awareness. This is the number of the person who has just begun to realise that in addition to the past and the present, there is also another idea called the future. He begins to see that there are consequences to actions. The beginnings of this awareness naturally generate the dangers of impatience. In very simple terms, it is like a child who sees something it wants for the first time, but recognises that it lies in the future, just out of reach. So coupled with the beginnings of future sight must also come the cultivation of patience, or feeding the present in order to fortify for the future.

The person whose Karmic root is 5 must always come to terms with the present in order to cope with his vision and his potential.

51

Step One: Hexagram 48 (The Well)

The inferior man is capable of hitting absolute rock bottom in terms of social usefulness. The superior man who feels justified in detaching himself from the affairs of the everyday world may still be useful in a higher sense to society through the cultivation of the spirit. The extreme opposite of this is represented in the inferior man's total lack of recognition of any spiritual ideal. Such a failure can drive the inferior man into a spiritual void without even hope left.

Step Two: Hexagram 39 (Impasse: Difficult Obstacles)

The superior man never wilfully seeks conflict, neither does he court dangerous situations or people. The inferior man does not recognise this principle and either deliberately sets out to cause trouble, or blunders into it unknowingly. However, when the superior man is confronted by a dangerous situation which goes beyond any personal threat to himself and endangers those who are under his care, he has no choice but to meet the danger in order to avert it before it harms those who are defenceless. The superior man is always reluctant to allow such a situation even to develop, but there are times when circumstances force his hand – even then he acts in such a way as to cause the minimum of harm. He restrains rather than attacks.

Step Three: Hexagram 8 (Leadership and Initiative)

The superior man is never arrogant. When he wishes to understand a new situation or has dealings with strangers, he first makes himself receptive by opening himself up to the new influence. The inferior man does not do this. He presumes he understands the situation and he rushes in to impose his view upon it. Thus the superior man reprimands the inferior man for such vulgarity.

The situation pictured is highly complex. The inferior man, through his impatience, thinks it is simple and thereby creates, quite unnecessarily, a spiral of misunderstandings. This is the essence of the soap opera. The opposite is also true – a simple situation can be made to seem convoluted and complicated.

The inferior man makes it extremely difficult for himself to come under the guidance of the superior man because he is under the delusion that he understands the situation when he does not. The problem for the superior man, and this is the essential problem, is communicating to the inferior man the complications which arise from the inferior man's convoluted way of thinking.

Step Four: Hexagram 45 (The Group)

The superior man works because he values the work itself. He works from a spirit of altruism. The inferior man is motivated by material reward and public praise and works to those ends. He measures his value as an individual in terms of his material possessions, in terms of his bank balance and his public profile. The superior man is recognised for his work alone.

Step Five: Hexagram 16 (Enthusiasm (Music))

Enthusiasm is a vital and valuable personal quality, and only under very special and rare circumstances can anyone be justified in deliberately dampening it in another. Normally, enthusiasm finds its own level and is appropriate to the circumstances because when someone is enthusiastic, they are resonating with the higher energies in the environment. However, where enthusiasm is allowed to go to excess, it can harm the superior man, and so he is justified in containing it, for which the inferior man is later grateful as he avoids regret.

Step Six: Hexagram 35 (Progress)

Once again, this Karmic progression underlines a pattern in which the inferior man is brought under the control of the superior man through being taught the idea of what is appropriate enthusiasm, or appropriate force, or appropriate restraint, or appropriate discrimination.

The inferior man is volatile and full of energy, and has a tendency to allow himself to become over-excited, and so lose the capacity to resonate 'appropriately' with the superior man. Until he learns this lesson, or rather, understands how to tune himself better, he will constantly encounter situations which put this capacity to the test.

Synthesis

The other side of the coin is that the superior man who knows that the secret of resonating with other people is in first being receptive to them, can then orchestrate whatever melody he likes.

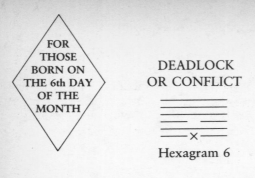

FOR
THOSE
BORN ON
THE 6th DAY
OF THE
MONTH

DEADLOCK
OR CONFLICT

Hexagram 6

> *Your Karmic number is 6 (Earth-oriented). Without a secure home base, you are unhappy. Whatever your other strengths – a highly developed musical discrimination and taste, a love of 'high' culture, a tendency to philosophising, and a slight preoccupation with health matters – your life only works if your home is secure. All your other qualities cannot prosper without this.*

YOUR ROOT HEXAGRAM: HEXAGRAM 6

Your root hexagram gives the climate or ambience of the six Karmic pictures which are the principal characteristics of your Karmic journey.

Karmic root 6 symbolises the discovery of a different point of view, the awareness that others may disagree with you and the awareness that you may disagree with them. This is therefore the number of conflict, discourse and argument at this level in the spiral of consciousness. The Karmic number 6 enshrines within it the dawnings of the ability to distinguish different states of mind, the first awareness that there is more than one possible perspective in any objective view. To overcome the difficulties inherent in such realisations, you must learn to think carefully through the different points of view before you adopt any one of them. The value in this is that you avoid unnecessary conflict by learning to appreciate the validity of different perspectives. If this lesson is learned well, you can never be accused of narrow-mindedness and you have the possibility of learning a total perspective eventually: that is the ability to appreciate and understand all the possible perspectives around a particular subject of contemplation. The extreme of failing to learn this lesson is the bigot. You are recommended to read widely from the literature of many cultures from many periods of history in order to appreciate the sheer breadth of possible points of view.

Step One: Hexagram 10 (Sincerity)

The superior man does not allow himself to be dazzled by the rewards of the glamour world. He recognises that much that is qualitative in life is reflected and released through artistic endeavours. He also recognises that those artists who express their perception of the quality of life in the public eye are often surrounded or presented to the public through the gloss and tinsel of the commercial filter. But he is not deceived by this. The superior man always perceives the quality and retains his integrity even if he becomes such a public figure himself. The inferior man is completely taken in and duped into seeking the rewards of such a position while losing sight of the quality of the work.

Step Two: Hexagram 25 (Innocence)

The superior man is always capable of living entirely in the present. That is to say, his actions are capable of being permeated and suffused by a certain vigour and energy which the inferior man can never attain because he always acts with his eye on the morrow. For the inferior man, nothing is worth doing for itself. The superior man is capable of work for its own sake, and not just to secure the future.

Step Three: Hexagram 13 (Peace)

The Karmic picture is of an integrated social situation of any scale from the family unit through to the local community, the national identity and the world as one family. The superior man is never misguided in his loyalties to the extent that he acts in a destructive way where the 'social group' as a whole is at stake. The inferior man mistrusts the ideal of successful social integration and identifies himself with those who feel the same way, with the result that successful social integration is seriously impeded by his actions. He is also under the misapprehension that his identity with such a group furthers the aims of the social unit as a whole, on whatever scale that is understood.

The inferior man's signature is to entertain ideas that the superior man is not superior at all. In this way, the inferior man isolates himself from the superior man. Where the inferior man and the superior man are so extremely separated, we have a picture of a schizophrenic personality. Expressed in global terms, we have a schizophrenic world. However, this condition is *not* static.

Step Four: Hexagram 37 (The Family)

This situation concerns domestic finance and management. The superior and the inferior do not come into conflict here. They agree that the most desirable situation is where income equals expenditure.

Step Five: Hexagram 22 (Grace, Aesthetics)

The Karmic theme emerges still more strongly here where the view of the superior man is underlined with regard to the ideas or conflict between the pursuit of material wealth and the implied cosiness and comfort that that can bring, and the infinitely more valuable spiritual or qualitative achievement. It is the Karma of this person to experience this conflict and to resolve it. The inferior man does not perceive even the idea of spiritual treasures but the superior man lives for nothing else. The superior man, therefore, attracts to himself people of like mind, those who value and treasure the quality side of life, and he is unhappy if he is unable to be with his own kind.

There is a fundamental law of the Tao for which the *I Ching* is a huge metaphor: *like attracts like*. Everything has resonance and vibration. We are attracted to those who, in a perfectly natural way, resonate on our frequency. And in time to come mankind will develop a vast and integrated science based around that key concept of resonance.

Step Six: Hexagram 36 (The Encroaching Shadow)

The inferior man is naturally antagonistic towards the superior man. This antagonism can sometimes be so violent and extreme that the superior man is unable to bring the inferior man under any kind of reasonable restraint. The superior man knows that if he cannot do this there is no hope of communicating the way of the Tao to the inferior man, so he withdraws to the point where the inferior man cannot touch him at all; the superior man becomes invisible to the inferior man and leaves him entirely on his own.

What is the effect of such a course of action on the part of the superior man? The inferior man, having no one to fight, either becomes quiet and ceases to be violent and antagonistic, and thereby becomes receptive and accessible to the superior man once more, or he turns his anger and aggression on himself, thereby destroying himself. However, the superior man cannot be destroyed.

Synthesis

Your Karmic challenges can be summarised as the drive to penetrate everything that is superficial and reach the level of qualitative experience and self-expression through any form with which you feel you can resonate best. Your aptitude to be a leading light in any one of the scales of social settings described above (this is a matter of personal energy) is singular and pronounced.

ARMY:
CHALLENGE/SELF-CONTROL

FOR
THOSE
BORN ON
THE 7th DAY
OF THE
MONTH

Hexagram 7

> *Your Karmic number is 7 (Heaven-oriented). Seven is traditionally regarded as a divine number and so it tends to be characterised in people as the drive towards perfection. It is also the number of the psychic or clairvoyant. For such people, meditation is a natural process – they do it without ceremony. You are very often difficult to get on with, as you can be over-critical. You need deeply challenging intellectual pursuits.*

YOUR ROOT HEXAGRAM: HEXAGRAM 7

Your root hexagram gives the climate or ambience of the six Karmic pictures which are the principal characteristics of your Karmic journey.

The inherent Karmic challenge here is the formation of purpose. Implicit in the idea of working out a strategy or a scheme to follow in life is the marshalling of your energies and bringing into focus all the facets of your personality in order to achieve momentum and direction and in order to overcome challenges. The implication of this number is that you will be confronted with challenges which will draw upon all your talents, all your energies, but this does not mean to say that the employment of all your talents and energies will necessarily lead you to victory. What is required is your ability to organise your inner resources in the best possible way. The essence of your Karmic challenge is to learn to plan and to be strategic so that you can make the best and most economical use of your resources.

Step One: Hexagram 19 (The Open Door)

The inferior man seeks to manipulate people and to ingratiate himself into the company of those who also seek to manipulate people. The superior man, by his very nature, and often unintentionally, influences people and causes in order to further their alignment with the superior way. The inferior man possesses no such concept.

The superior man may often be invited to work in such a way as to bring beneficial influence to bear on a cause. The point is that the superior man cannot help but influence by example, because it is the inner law of his being. The inferior man's signature is that he thinks in terms of power over other people. This is not influence, but manipulation. The superior man understands that real power has kindness at its heart.

Step Two: Hexagram 24 (The Moment of Transition)

During times of transition, the inferior man draws closer to the superior man. The superior man recognises this as a willingness to be guided, therefore the inferior man is characterised by a greater humility which is the prerequisite for the inferior man in a time of transition, and assists in the smoothness of the transition.

Step Three: Hexagram 36 (The Encroaching Shadow)

The picture here is of a complex situation which has been brought about by a hidden but deep flaw. Something is very wrong. The superior man is aware only that the picture is out of alignment in its depiction of the superior way. Suddenly, due to a natural change, the superior man perceives, through the complications, the flaw. He acts swiftly in order to alter the nature of the inferior element so that it may, in time, evolve into alignment with the superior way.

His superiority consists of his awareness that the situation cannot be transformed in all its particulars in a single manoeuvre. The inferior man thinks he can change things overnight.

Step Four: Hexagram 55 (The Brimming Cup)

The superior man is in association with others of like disposition and they work closely together in order to propagate benefit for the wider social community. This is always pictured as a time of light and is characterised by a feeling of joy as there are no inferior elements present. Such a circumstance always follows a period of darkness such as one might experience during an eclipse of the sun.

Step Five: Hexagram 49 (Dynamism)

The superior man is always concerned with changes and improvements. He thinks deeply about these things until he perceives a way to release the influence of a new system. However, even before he discloses the details of his plan, the communication of his intentions has already taken place to the minds of those who are kindred by means of an as yet invisible resonance. Here we are picturing the possibility of great and momentous changes. When the superior man makes the details of his plan known in the conventional way, he meets with complete and unreserved support.

Step Six: Hexagram 13 (Peace)

The true work of the superior man is to further the higher aims of mankind, but the superior man cannot do this without an atmosphere of warmth and affection and co-operation from others of his kind.

Here the superior man recognises that circle of people with whom he has spiritual alignment and kindred aims. He knows that they are the same as him, but cannot enter the circle because their affection does not reach him, and his affection does not reach them. Thus the essential line of direct communication is missing. However, the superior man need have no cause for sorrow in this because, providing he adheres to the superior way, a path will naturally open.

Synthesis

The Karmic path describes the superior man's quality of influence in the realisation of the higher aims of mankind. Whatever sphere of influence opens up for you, it will bring great benefit to others, even those you do not know personally. Your Karmic path is to help bring individuals and organisations into alignment with the superior way. Everything you do should bear this hallmark.

FOR
THOSE
BORN ON
THE 8th DAY
OF THE
MONTH

LEADERSHIP

Hexagram 8

> *Your Karmic number is 8 (Earth-oriented). You have a knack for big business. You will have a very close relationship with very large sums of money. You will either earn it or manage it or in some way influence its acquisition or expenditure. You are something of a showman. Properly developed, you can display a fine and balanced judgment of complex situations (artistic, business, etc.). Your creativity and spontaneity can only flourish within some kind of formal structure. This could be of your own design.*

YOUR ROOT HEXAGRAM: HEXAGRAM 8

Your root hexagram gives the climate or ambience of the six Karmic pictures which are the principal characteristics of your Karmic journey.

If all else is to flow smoothly throughout your life, then your most vital Karmic challenge is to find your centre of gravity. This is the spiritual focus which harmonises your personality and character. It is only from this point that you are able to hold yourself together and to make progress. From the centre (and this may be quite simply the ability to act 100 per cent from the heart) you can handle diversity with success. This single idea holds the secret of your ability to lead.

66

Step One: Hexagram 3 (Difficult Beginnings)

The picture is of obstacles and difficulties at the beginning of a period of prolonged activity. The inferior man, because of the seriousness of the difficulties, easily loses his way. He meanders off the path of his Karma. He may be viewed as something of an experimentalist, but this is a false view of one who has lost his way and appears to be exploring the abundant opportunities and possibilities which he can perceive. Only when the inferior man recognises that – despite his adaptability and vast potential in a number of lines of activity – can he realise the true path of his Karma by ultimately deferring to the superior man who is able to show him the superior way. If the inferior man actively seeks the guidance of the superior man, he will overcome his initial difficulties.

Step Two: Hexagram 60 (Limitation/Discrimination)

The road of Karma is now clear. The superior man recognises his opportunity to act without distraction or interference from the inferior man and the outside world. He seizes this moment to act and thereby achieves his aims.

Step Three: Hexagram 5 (Patience)

Both the inferior man and the superior man may not be of one will, but they contemplate the same object. The picture is one of expectancy, anticipation, very much like the attitude of a predatory cat concealed in the bushes with its eyes fixed on the kill.

The superior man knows the precise moment to strike because he is aware of the wider view and can see the whole landscape. He understands the value of patience. The inferior man sees only the kill.

Here, due to the impatience of the inferior man, he strikes a fraction of a second too soon, and the superior man cannot prevent it. The inferior man has leaped into a trap laid for his kill instead of waiting for his prey to move beyond the sphere of danger. Only by deferring to the superior man can the inferior man extricate himself now.

Step Four: Hexagram 43 (Personal Resolution)

The inferior man and the superior man are in profound disagreement as to which is the correct path to follow. The superior man makes the correct path very clear to the inferior man, but the inferior man refuses to listen. He is obstinate, stubborn, arrogant and self-willed. The superior man is flexible, but adamant. The feeling between them is one of great discomfort. But still the inferior man is convinced that he is right and the superior man is wrong. The superior man considers the option of remaining silent until the inferior man's obstinacy dissipates.

Step Five: Hexagram 14 (Wealth)

The superior man is kindhearted. If he is in a position to be benevolent, he is benevolent, but he does not allow his benevolent intentions to cancel themselves out through unnecessary interference and insensitivity to others. The inferior man is not aware of the effects his acts of kindness may have and does not know that sometimes an act of benevolence may be interpreted as disrespect. The superior man knows how to give without offending.

Step Six: Hexagram 34 (Leading Initiative)

The inferior man has committed his act. He has made his mistake and he is in trouble. His first thought is to panic and to struggle and to attempt to flee. The superior man knows that the inferior man is trapped and that any attempt to escape is a pointless waste of energy. The superior man also sees that the way out will make itself apparent, and that all he has to do is keep perfectly still and calm until the time to escape is right. The superior man also knows that this is not only the correct course of action, but the only meaningful one.

Synthesis

You are a person of great potential. Although your beginnings may be confusing and disorienting, once your Karmic path has become known to you, you have a relatively clear road to achievement and you may fulfil yourself. This is sometimes called success. The intersections of your Karma imply a warm and expansive disposition which for a wealthy person also suggests a powerful urge towards philanthropy. The only thing you have to learn is the art of giving without humiliating.

LIMITED PERSUASION

Hexagram 9

> *Your Karmic number is 9 (Heaven-oriented). You have a mind capable of a broad philosophical outlook. You view the world as a whole and you tend, through your experience, to become worldly-wise. You will probably be acclaimed in some field. During your early years, people will take advantage of your innate generosity, but this won't harm you. Nine is the number of world knowledge.*

YOUR ROOT HEXAGRAM: HEXAGRAM 9

Your root hexagram gives the climate or ambience of the six Karmic pictures which are the principal characteristics of your Karmic journey.

The essence of the Karmic challenge which permeates all your endeavours in life is your ability to handle unruly and intractable forces arising not only within yourself but also in others. Since you lack the strength to entirely overcome the forces of chaos, you nevertheless have the power to act in a way which has the same effect: you can appease, you can suggest, imply, hint, persuade in a very diplomatic way. The art here is not to confront or meet forces head on. Your talent is adaptability. If you nurture your ability to work with these intractable forces by being adaptable (unruly or chaotic forces have no self-control, and therefore cannot be adaptable), you will possess the key advantage. This is what is meant by 'The Taming Power of the Small'. It is your ability to contain situations with very little energy available.

71

Step One: Hexagram 57 (The Impressionable)

The inferior man avoids all responsibility for taking decisions which have a direct bearing on the quality of his life. He has a 'take it or leave it' attitude ('Easy come, easy go'). Thus, even when it seems to him that a decision needs to be made, he will not make that decision or take that initiative. He can be very wishy-washy in his view of the world. The result may be that his life will start to lose definition around the edges. He will become vague and blurred in his view of the world.

The superior man is never obnoxiously forceful, but he does not shy away from taking the initiative or making clear-cut decisions. The superior man never allows the inferior man to dictate terms to him, but will quietly and definitely take control of the situation.

Step Two: Hexagram 53 (Development (Gradual Progress))

The situation pictures a period just after a transition has been achieved, and therefore this is a period of new adjustment. The inferior man does not trust the new situation entirely, and he allows doubts to creep in which may harm his confidence. The superior man translates these feelings into an attitude of caution and accepts confidently the responsibilities which the new landscape presents and perceives the opportunity to expand his field of activity in a happy mood.

Step Three: Hexagram 20 (View of the World)

In order for the inferior man to reconcile himself with the superior man, he cannot escape a period in his life which is devoted to self-examination or the exploration of the inner landscape. The inferior man cannot undertake this work in a positive spirit without the direct guidance and involvement of the superior man, but as this period represents a natural cycle in the inferior man's life, there is nothing else to do but this and so it is easy for the superior and inferior elements to interlock successfully. The result is an expansion of spiritual awareness or self-improvement of the whole person, and its ultimate value is in the effect of such a renewed person upon others.

Every increase in self-awareness represents an increase for the superior man and therefore an increase in clarity and creative potential. This means increased energy.

Step Four: Hexagram 12 (Superficiality/Stagnation/Standstill)

The natural cycle requires that stillness evolves into movement. This pictures the eyes of the inferior man turned from his contemplation of the superior man to the outside world of action. The superior man, so to speak, looks through the eyes of the inferior man in order to find an appropriate field of activity. If the superior man seeks a position or field of action in the world, others will recognise him and support him, and he will find his right place naturally. Thus co-operation comes to the superior man. The inferior man is liable to make mistakes if he is not properly guided as to his correct field of action.

Step Five: Hexagram 35 (Progress)

The Karmic picture is that of a clear road. Faced with such a prospect, the superior man knows that he must proceed without delay in order to gain headway. This stretch of the road is rarely taken in isolation. Thus the superior man makes progress with his companions, with whom he shares a common path. This stretch of the road is also in the view of a wider social group. The presence of the superior man in this part of his Karmic journey has an uplifting and beneficial influence on many other people. Due to the absence of any negative influences from the inferior man, the superior man is able to bear the burdens of other people as if they are his own and with no apparent effort.

Step Six: Hexagram 16 (Enthusiasm/Music/Religious Force)

The inferior man is liable to misjudge the situation and believe that he has an advantage where he has none. This is not a gross error, but it is likely to be expressed in over-zealousness. If he pushes this too far, quite apart from feeling embarrassed, he might do some harm to the superior man. Knowing this, the superior man restrains such enthusiasm before it becomes uncontrollable and therefore all harm is forestalled.

The superior man, on the other hand, is able to resonate perfectly with any situation and so knows how to act appropriately.

Synthesis

The superior man prospers when he takes the world view. The inferior man can find no durable meaning to his actions because he does not take the world view.

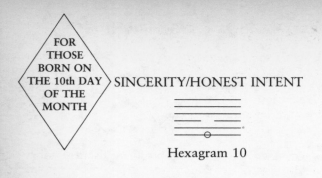

FOR
THOSE
BORN ON
THE 10th DAY
OF THE
MONTH

SINCERITY/HONEST INTENT

Hexagram 10

Your Karmic number is 10 (Earth-oriented). Once you have found your feet, you are quite capable of standing on them unassisted and unaided. You are happiest working independently of others and rarely will you be drawn into equal partnerships. As an individualist you are capable of taking on responsibilities, and if you cultivate this ability you can lead. Be prepared to take risks and have a little more courage in unusual situations. Don't hedge all your bets.

YOUR ROOT HEXAGRAM: HEXAGRAM 10

Your root hexagram gives the climate or ambience of the six Karmic pictures which are the principal characteristics of your Karmic journey.

Your Karmic root emphasises a talent to be pleasant, charming and perfectly mannered. This is a quality you must develop to the very highest level as there is no other way in which you can bring your influence to bear when surrounded by people who have no self-control and behave in a wild and unruly fashion. Your Karmic challenge is to learn how to bring these potentially dangerous situations under control by the force of your behaviour which is able to set unruly people an example. You should understand that it is the quality of your conduct that is the example you set and it is from this alone that your ability to control intemperate people arises. Distinguish this from powers of persuasion and the subtleties of diplomacy. People may not always like you, but they will admire you in a special way.

76

Step One: Hexagram 6 (Deadlock)

The superior man does not indulge in personal insults, neither does he allow differences of opinion to escalate to the point where communication breaks down. The inferior man cannot distinguish between an objective viewpoint and a subjective attitude unless it is pointed out by the superior man. The superior man forgives and does not indulge in injured retorts. The inferior man can hold a grudge.

Step Two: Hexagram 12 (Superficiality)

The superior man can sustain difficult and arduous periods if he is sure that his work helps the inferior man. The inferior man will, however, put the superior man to the test, and providing the superior man does not compromise his clarity or his integrity, the inferior man is constantly challenged to come up to standard. If the arduous period is withstood in this way, success must be the outcome.

Step Three: Hexagram 33 (Strategic Retreat/Withdrawal)

The superior man has been placed in the most profoundly

disquieting compromise by the inferior man. The superior man had no choice in the matter and could not avoid it. The situation is almost, but not quite, hopeless. The superior man never defers to the inferior man except in an almost life-and-death situation. In order to save the inferior man from himself, the superior man is here forced to make a concession against his own better judgment. For the superior man, the situation is completely unsatisfactory, but because it was unavoidable it has to be tolerated. The outcome is uncertain.

Step Four: Hexagram 53 (Development/Gradual Progress)

The Karmic path continues very much in the same vein. The superior and inferior are in an uncomfortable relationship which the superior man would not have chosen for himself, but which in the natural course of things was destined. The inevitability of the superior man's path compels him to make the best of things. In the absence of an alternative route, the superior man knows how to make the best of a situation, and teaches the inferior man through the inevitable difficulties how to develop himself personally. The superior man regards this as a challenge.

At the end of the difficulties, a new path will suggest itself to the superior man which is more appropriate to his qualities and to which he will feel more suited.

Step Five: Hexagram 52 (Learning to Relax)

In personal matters especially, the superior man thinks carefully before he speaks so that he will have no need to regret his words. The inferior man speaks before he considers carefully the effect his words will have, and so may cause embarrassment or offence or bring about a complicated misunderstanding.

Step Six: Hexagram 15 (Modesty)

The superior man is naturally modest and this is evident in his actions. The superior man can distinguish between true modesty and false modesty in others. The inferior man is immodest and boastful in his actions. The inferior man may use a naturally modest disposition as an excuse for not doing anything. He feels his actions would make too strong a statement to be 'modest'. The superior man does whatever is necessary and he does it modestly. This is true modesty.

Synthesis

This Karmic route is not the easiest as the superior man is beset with difficulties which are not of his choosing. He is yoked for a period of his Karmic journey to an inferior man who lacks initiative, but the superior man is able to keep an even keel, though he often feels he is being put to a lot of trouble for nothing. He may well be pleasantly surprised.

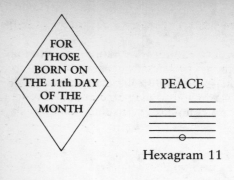

FOR
THOSE
BORN ON
THE 11th DAY
OF THE
MONTH

PEACE

Hexagram 11

> *Your Karmic number is 11 (Heaven-oriented). You have a great deal of energy. You therefore conceive lofty ambitions in order to fulfil yourself. In order to be successful, you must believe in your inspiration. Your intellectual capabilities leave nothing to be desired, but if they are superseded by your intuitive abilities, you cannot fail.*

YOUR ROOT HEXAGRAM: HEXAGRAM 11

Your root hexagram gives the climate or ambience of the six Karmic pictures which are the principal characteristics of your Karmic journey.

Your challenge is to cultivate inner tranquillity. Since 'Peace' is your Karmic root, all your success stems from your ability to remain calm and composed within yourself. This is such a positive beginning because all the forces are beautifully balanced, and thus there is great scope for unhindered success and beneficial action. If you remember that the most harmful thing you can do to yourself is to lose your temper then the way to notable success can be yours.

Step One: Hexagram 46 (Beginning of Ascent)

The superior man is in total control of his destiny. The inferior man presents no obstacles. Therefore the Karmic road to achievement starts with a clear advantage. The superior man has no trouble in attracting like-minded companions to support him and to help him on his way. He is therefore destined to make his mark in the world.

Step Two: Hexagram 15 (Modesty)

There is no conflict between the superior and the inferior man. The superior man always acts from the heart and is therefore truly modest. When there is no conflict between the superior and inferior, the superior man's influence is multiplied and impresses others deeply.

Step Three: Hexagram 2 (The Receptive)

The inferior man is afraid that his work will not be recognised and praised. He therefore seeks to be recognised and acknowledged. Taken to extremes, the inferior man will, in a fit of egocentric frenzy, deliberately court the public gaze, and will privately throw tantrums if he is ignored. The superior man lets his work speak for itself, confident that if it has merit, it will be recognised.

Step Four: Hexagram 16 (Music/Enthusiasm)

There is no conflict between the superior and the inferior man. This reinforces the total energy of the superior man engaged in work. He is viewed by others as completely positive and such enthusiasm naturally engages co-operation from others. The total absence of doubt imbues the superior man's activities with an unfaltering magic. Great achievements must follow if such positive energy can be sustained.

Step Five: Hexagram 45 (The Group)

When the superior man finds his line of activity he applies himself with dedication and develops a resilience to difficulties in such a way that the progress of the work is unstoppable. The superior man invested with this dedication becomes the example of the correct attitude for those whom he leads or influences. The inferior man is willing to follow the superior man in order to learn dedication. He can only learn this through working with the superior man.

Step Six: Hexagram 12 (Superficiality)

Part of the natural cycle in the outpourings of energy are periods of slumps, or blocks. These natural stops in the flow can cause the inferior man to abandon the work. Only the superior man can start the flow again. Only the energy of the superior man perseveres and sees things through to completion. The superior man is never defeated. The inferior man is easily defeated. The superior man can restore dynamic activity in a period of stagnation. The inferior man cannot stop him.

Synthesis

This Karmic road is bright and full of great promise. You are disposed towards hard work and therefore the fulfilment of your aspirations. Because the accent here is on co-operation from other people, rather than impediments, your Karmic road is destined to be favoured, and your work recognised. It is also possible that your work will outlive you.

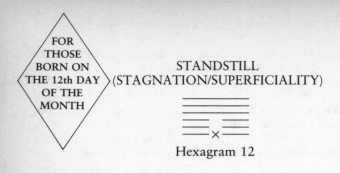

STANDSTILL
(STAGNATION/SUPERFICIALITY)

Hexagram 12

Your Karmic number is 12 (Earth-oriented). You have quite definite and pronounced literary leanings. You could develop this propensity. It is vital that your close personal relationships are happy, otherwise your other talents, especially your social charms, do not shine. But your practical turn of mind rarely deserts you. You could be fastidious, a stickler for details.

YOUR ROOT HEXAGRAM: HEXAGRAM 12

Your root hexagram gives the climate or ambience of the six Karmic pictures which are the principal characteristics of your Karmic journey.

The meaning of your Karmic root is concerned with the timing of your actions and projects. The essence of the principle which you have to be aware of throughout your life is when *not* to act. It could be that you will avoid many difficulties and frustrations if you learn to tune yourself with events to such an extent that you can intuitively understand when your actions will bear no fruit. It follows that once you have learned to read the signs of the times as they affect your personal challenges, your sense of timing will become perfected so that you only engage your energies when you know that you are going to get somewhere. Initially, this is only something you can learn through experience.

Learning the art of tuning with the environment at its more spiritual level will eventually become a matter of intuition for you. You will, in effect, be able to divine motivations of the people you are required to deal with and you will learn to perfect the art of when to make your move. The hexagram is about coping with the idea of inactivity. This is why it is called 'Standstill' or 'Stagnation'. If you know why you are not acting (i.e. because it is the wrong time to act), it is because you have chosen not to oppose the Tao. This is standing still. If you do not know why it is that your actions have no effect, then this is something you experience as stagnation, a completely different idea. This crucial distinction will characterise much of your Karmic journey and it is well for you to bear it in mind.

Step One: Hexagram 25 (Innocence)

The superior man is not afraid to take the initiative when the time is right. The inferior man does not know when the time is right. He waits for events to happen to him. The superior man acts upon the world. When it is appropriate he takes control of events. There is no quarrel between the superior and the inferior man and so action is possible.

Step Two: Hexagram 10 (Sincerity (Honest Intent))

The superior man is sincere and honest even in those times when the inferior man is deluded into believing that it is more comfortable to allow events to distract him. The superior man sees his path of Karma clearly and has the strength to follow it. The inferior man prefers to lean on the initiatives of others. The superior man is prepared to take leave of the inferior man as an act of self-honesty if this is the only way of demonstrating to the inferior man that he will not be distracted from his true path no matter what. The inferior man is therefore compelled to follow the superior man.

Step Three: Hexagram 1 (Creativity)

Here is pictured a period of transition wherein the superior man is elevated to a suitable position of influence which accords with his nature. At such times the inferior man indulges in regrets of past mistakes. He dwells upon frustrations, lists resentments, indulges in bitterness. The superior man never allows his energy to be misused in this way, especially at a time which follows an important transition. The superior man always recognises the propitiousness of the time and takes advantage of it to make headway.

Step Four: Hexagram 9 (Limited Persuasion)

It is only natural that in difficult situations the inferior man should ask the superior man for help and advice. This is a very special circumstance which honours both the inferior man and the superior man, for usually the superior man in difficult times takes the initiative to intervene in order to avoid serious mistakes. Thus the superior man, who is never flattered, feels it his duty to give such advice as he knows to be crucial to the inferior man because he knows the inferior man will act upon it, and will have to bear the consequences of his actions.

Step Five: Hexagram 26 (Held in Check)

When the inferior man is confronted by a force or a threat from outside, his first thought is to defend himself from its effects. The inferior man thinks of protection as a way of overcoming the force. The superior man knows that he cannot measure or control any force which attacks him without understanding its source. Thus the superior man concentrates his energies on neutralising the unwanted force at its source. Thus he has no need to protect himself. The superior man never wastes his energy in deploying it for defence. He prevents the attack by penetrating to the source of the aggression and neutralising it there. The inferior man invites mistrust by defending himself. The inferior man does not know that a) he cannot defend himself from the superior man and b) that he has no need to protect himself from the superior man. The superior man offers to harm nobody.

Step Six: Hexagram 11 (Peace)

The superior man is under attack from the inferior man. The reflex action of the inferior man in the superior man's position would be to defend and retaliate. When the superior man does not have the necessary force to overcome the inferior man's attack, all he can do is to accept it. Where the inferior man is in control, chaos rules. All the superior man can do is to withdraw into himself.

This situation can be understood in terms of the superior man who is compelled to watch the inferior man wantonly destroy all that is good and valuable in life in the full knowledge that he is helpless to prevent it. This is a sad state of affairs in the opinion of the superior man.

Synthesis

The superior man is clear about his path. Although the inferior man is wilful, he rarely has the opportunity to take control over events. Only in one instance does the inferior man make his destructive influence felt in the superior man's life, and for you this has a continuing influence which you feel you cannot afford to ignore.

FOR
THOSE
BORN ON
THE 13th DAY
OF THE
MONTH

FELLOWSHIP WITH MEN
(PEACE IN THE WORLD)

Hexagram 13

*Your Karmic number is 13 (Heaven-oriented). You have a
great aptitude for understanding the physical world
according to mechanical and scientific laws. It is easy for
you to perceive structure and you have a strong aptitude
for organising ideas and people. In order to balance this
perception you should practise and cultivate those arts
which express your more personal feelings — painting,
drawing, musical composition or playing a musical
instrument, generally working with your hands. Think
about the meaning of love more often.*

YOUR ROOT HEXAGRAM: HEXAGRAM 13

Your root hexagram gives the climate or ambience of the six
Karmic pictures which are the principal characteristics of your
Karmic journey.

Those with this Karmic root are advised that their actions
will have all the more meaning and clarity if they think in terms
of universal ideas as opposed to partisan or factionalistic
persuasions. The source of your strength lies in being the
yielding centre within a strong structure. That is to say, if you
try to impose your will in a hard and fast way while holding a
central position of authority, you run the risk of fracturing the
whole structure. This is why you are required to take the widest
possible view of your position. Clarity means clear definition of
aims. This is only possible when you perceive situations as
wholes. At your highest level of action, you are a unifier. You
can bring people and situations into co-operation. You have the

capacity, providing you are yielding in nature, to inspire in others the will to unity and action. This is why the hexagram is called 'Fellowship with Men'. It pictures a universal state of mankind which I call 'Peace in the World'.

You can be a truly effective leader if you are enlightened as to the integrating and unifying aspirations of mankind. That is to say, you can achieve success at any level through life if you become a symbol and exponent of co-operation as opposed to competition. If you become an exponent of competition, you will set up divisive forces in life and move further away from the ideal of unitive action or peace in the world. You were born to help the cause of co-operation.

Step One: Hexagram 33 (Retreat, Strategic Withdrawal)

The inferior man is alone and without guidance. The superior man has withdrawn. When this happens, the inferior man is in danger. The only thing he can do is to keep perfectly still and desist from any kind of movement or intention. The situation here is that the inferior man has blundered into a trap which the superior man warned against. The inferior man, in his stillness, will recognise the nature of his predicament and this will serve as the best possible warning against a recurrence.

The inferior man must learn foresight in matters of life and death.

Step Two: Hexagram 44 (Meeting)

When the superior man finds himself in the company of oppressive and obnoxious influences, he withdraws from them entirely. If he cannot do this by physically removing himself he withdraws into deep inner silence, thereby cutting the influence off so that it cannot harm him. The inferior man, when confronted with exactly the same situation, tries to rid himself of this influence by emotional outbursts or by angry and violent means. The malevolent influence is excited and engaged by the inferior man's reaction and thus its power over the inferior man is increased and the power of the inferior man is proportionately decreased. The superior man knows that the only way to treat such an unwholesome influence is as a doctor would a disease – he cuts it off so that it does not spread.

Step Three: Hexagram 6 (Deadlock)

The situation pictured here is that of work, any work, done, completed. The superior man takes his work sufficiently seriously so that it bears his authentic mark. If someone were to plagiarise or steal the superior man's work and pass it off as his own, and succeed in making others believe that it is his own – something only an inferior man would do – the superior man would not be in the least concerned. It is enough that the superior man has done the work himself, and since he knows that the work came from him, it can never truthfully be lost to him. It is, in a real sense, his work, and this is enough for the superior man. The inferior man would in these circumstances be indignant, upset and outraged, and would seek official recognition for his stolen work. It is not enough for the inferior man that the work stands done, for he does not understand that it cannot be lost to him.

Step Four: Hexagram 59 (Dispersion)

The inferior and the superior are not in conflict. The picture is of the superior man who perceives his Karmic road stretching out clearly before him. He sees a far-off goal, a special prize which must be won on behalf of humanity, a gift of knowledge. The superior man weighs and balances personal loyalties and understands that it is necessary to make some personal sacrifice if the goal is to be reached, the prize is to be won. The superior man realises that this can only be justified when the vision is clear and strong and worthy of prolonged effort. Such choices are only ever offered to the superior man and thus they are never passed over lightly.

Step Five: Hexagram 4 (Inexperience of the Young/The Student)

The situation pictured here is of an inferior man who feels lost and alone. He has lost sight of the superior man, and worse, he has forgotten about his existence altogether. The inferior man is sincere and innocent, though profoundly in need of guidance. The superior man finds no difficulty in helping this kind of person and it is simply by the presence of the superior man that the inferior man gains a keen insight into his own nature. In such circumstances, a closer bond is created.

Step Six: Hexagram 7 (Challenge)

In special kinds of work, it is necessary to employ specialists if the work is to have a successful outcome. After success has been achieved, and there is an atmosphere of confidence in the team, it is the duty of the superior man to reward the members of the team adequately and in the appropriate currency. What is appropriate is a matter of judgment in the superior man. As the superior man's perception embraces the whole situation in a clear perspective, he does not allow himself to become intoxicated by success to the extent that he rewards the team in inappropriate currency. Here the inferior man rewards the team with privilege, position and power. The superior man recognises that this is inappropriate and dangerous and does not flow from the nature of the work done.

Synthesis

The person who is travelling this Karmic road will encounter many fluctuations of fortune. However, if you understand the way of the superior man thoroughly enough, you can avoid misfortune which lies on the Karmic path because you will be able to recognise it for what it is. Your principal Karmic lesson is to look where you are going, take the wider view. You will have golden opportunities to do this, and the effects could be miraculous if you take heed. If you do not use your vision (in every sense of the word), you will always be bumping into things you could have avoided, and this will needlessly impair the quality of your life.

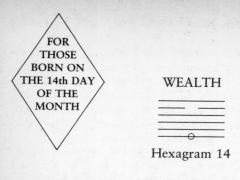

FOR
THOSE
BORN ON
THE 14th DAY
OF THE
MONTH

WEALTH

Hexagram 14

> *Your Karmic number is 14 (Earth-oriented). You could be something of a visionary, though you may find your insights difficult to apply. Without a solid working base your considerable energy is easily dissipated, so for success you need an established home. Among your many gifts, you are graced with a keen mind capable of great insights, but you also have breadth of mind, imagination. You love a good mystery. Your abilities shine most when you are methodical in your approach to problems. Perhaps you can be too self-absorbed.*

YOUR ROOT HEXAGRAM: HEXAGRAM 14

Your root hexagram gives the climate or ambience of the six Karmic pictures which are the principal characteristics of your Karmic journey.

You will find yourself handling large sums of money or resources for the benefit of the wider community. This may be wealth that you yourself have generated through your own enterprises in the commercial field, or wealth which by virtue of your office or responsibility is yours to disperse according to the terms of reference of your position. Since the disposal of material resources in a fair and equitable way is a vital aspect of the well-being of others, you have to be especially careful not to abuse this honour. Since great power is implied, the 'Karmic backlash' would be equally powerful if such a position were to be misused. The abuse of financial power is perhaps one of the greatest evils in the world.

The only way you can be sure of doing the right thing is to be guided by a higher light, which is why the *I Ching* says: 'Only in this way does he fulfil the benevolent will of God, who desires only good and not evil.' But first you have to overcome your biggest obstacle: before any favour is shown you by Fate you have to make an open and avowed *commitment* to serve your calling. Until then: nothing, only promises.

Step One: Hexagram 50 (The Cauldron (Valuable Work))

Spiritual matters are pictured here. The superior man recognises the time when he must concentrate his attentions entirely upon self-purification. The superior man contemplates the spirit, 'purges his soul of impurities'. The inferior man neglects his spiritual needs and makes no provision for basing his life on a foundation of clarity.

The focus for the superior man is on spiritual cleanliness, though for the inferior man this tendency may become an obsession with physical cleanliness.

This frame of action readily becomes comprehensible in well-known religious metaphors of sanctification, purification and so on, but meditative practices embrace the main ideas satisfactorily. The superior man does not neglect these.

Step Two: Hexagram 56 (The Traveller)

The superior man, even when in the company of strangers, and especially when travelling, retains inner calm. So stable is his inner calm, even in the midst of frenetic action, that people of less stable character are drawn to him irresistibly. People cannot but be attracted to real superiority. This invites the respect and admiration of others who are of like disposition. At such times, the superior man may form lasting friendships.

The inferior man, when confronted with the new and strange, loses his centre of gravity and therefore has no influence.

Step Three: Hexagram 35 (Progress)

There are times when even the superior man is impeded on his Karmic journey and requires the assistance of others. He knows first how to allow others to help him without compromising his integrity. While the superior man is able to rely on himself and is able to act independently, it takes real superiority to recognise those junctures in the road where independent action cannot lead to the goal and to accept help in good grace. For the superior man, such help does not ignite resentment, but reinforces his positive feeling. He is therefore empowered to continue until noteworthy progress has been realised.

The inferior man is arrogant. He thinks he can do it all by himself. He does not know how to recognise times when his progress depends on the goodwill and help of others and he takes no pride in the fact that he has attracted the help of superior men. His progress is therefore impeded.

Step Four: Hexagram 23 (Separation)

Even the superior man may experience completely untenable circumstances. Events coming from the outside have here entirely thwarted the superior man's power to make an impression on them. There is nothing the superior man can do personally to make an impression upon this unwholesome situation or to change it in any positive way. None of this affects his superiority, however. He merely accepts the circumstances as being beyond his control and even beyond his responsibility.

The superior man recognises that it is a waste of energy to fight circumstances over which he has no control. His superiority lies in his ability to submit, for the event has already happened.

Step Five: Hexagram 20 (A View of the World)

The superior man will have his superiority tested by the social community. He will be given great responsibilities wherein the care of others depends upon him. The superior man accepts such responsibilities willingly and releases the full force of his abilities in executing his duties. The superior man brings to bear the fruits of his self-knowledge for which he has suffered and worked so hard so that others may be shown an example and may benefit. The inferior man is not reckoned with here as he is entirely absent, and thus there is no conflict of duties. The superior man regards his work as a vocation and accepts nothing less of himself.

Step Six: Hexagram 8 (Leadership)

At certain junctures along the Karmic road, the superior man engages in dialogue with the inferior man about commitment to work. The inferior man recognises the situation and what is demanded of him but does not wish to commit himself to any action, for he doubts his own strength will endure. The superior man recognises the demands of the journey and wishes to commit himself as he has no doubts as to his strength and durability.

So long as this dialogue about commitment continues, the inferior man has his way, as no commitment can be made while the dialogue is taking place.

Synthesis

When your power of determination is expressed as a positive commitment to the service of others, you are able to make a staggering difference to the quality of their lives. Such a strong and kind influence is destined to endure.

MODESTY

Hexagram 15

> *Your Karmic number is 15 (Heaven-oriented). By nature you are a peace-loving person to whom competitiveness and antagonistic ways of behaving are alien. You are something of a romantic, an idealist, even a visionary and you express this in your appreciation of your environment. You have no fear of responsibility, but to shine you need a gentle, friendly companion with whom to share your life. You are oppressed by domineering, self-opinionated, noisy or violent people, and you must steer clear of them for your own peace of mind. Close and detailed work comes naturally to you. As an artist you may be brilliant. You can go too far in 'playing it safe', despite your talent for making successes out of challenges.*

YOUR ROOT HEXAGRAM: HEXAGRAM 15

Your root hexagram gives the climate or ambience of the six Karmic pictures which are the principal characteristics of your Karmic journey.

The meaning of your Karmic road is simple to express but difficult to endure: it is the preservation of a modest heart. Modesty is called 'the crown of a great man'. If you truly retain the spirit of modesty, no matter how great your achievements in life, they will not only shine, but they will endure through time. It is also the character of modesty to repel disintegrative forces. Modesty is therefore regarded as the finest attribute of the man of achievement.

Step One: Hexagram 36 (The Encroaching Shadow)

The superior man works hard without compromising his honesty and integrity. Even when this brings hardship and loss, insecurity and feelings of dejection, he does not veer from his path. He grits his teeth and endures it for he knows that these personal qualities are sovereign to his nature. This is real superiority.

The inferior man breaks down at the decisive moment. This is the difference between the superior and inferior man. The superior man is never distracted from the true course.

Step Two: Hexagram 11 (Peace)

The superior man is confronted by a clear Karmic road. He attracts the companionship and co-operation of other superior men. He sees with great clarity that he may bring his talents and his abilities to bear in full measure in order to make even uncertain situations yield a successful outcome. Here the superior man's energy is powerful and positive. He is able to show great vision and insight.

The superior man knows how to recognise a time when unswerving concentration will yield astounding results and he knows with whom he can work to make these benefits extend into the lives of others. The inferior man pictured here is held firmly in abeyance and offers no quarrel with the superior man.

In times of great co-operation, the inferior man cannot cope. He has no vision for the work and becomes preoccupied and enmeshed in taking sides with one group or another in order to stall. He may be over-critical of others and when pressed by the superior man will make excuses, once again in order to stall.

At such times the superior man maintains an even keel and steers an even, straight course. He does not procrastinate when the road is clear.

Step Three: Hexagram 19 (The Open Door)

When the superior man is showered with praises and gifts and is complimented with the offer of considerable responsibility, his attention becomes more keen, his concentration deeper, his awareness broader. Faced with exactly the same situation, the inferior man becomes arrogant, mean-spirited. He looks down his nose at other people, he deludes himself into thinking that he is the superior man. The superior man can see through all this as if it were transparent.

Step Four: Hexagram 54 (Marriage)

It is part of the fate of the superior man to meet those people who will be very special and close to him at the appointed time. Nothing can change that. The inferior man does not understand this, and therefore may be attracted to those people to whom he is not properly suited. Thus the people to whom he is suited cannot come close. The superior man will form a bond with the right person at the right time and he need have no fear or anxiety that this will not be so. Thus the superior man is rewarded for his patience and the inferior man pays for his impatience in this way.

Step Five: Hexagram 58 (Friendship)

The superior man knows without a doubt that the decisions he makes will have consequences and that he will have to live with those consequences. He knows the weight and importance of decisions that he makes at certain junctures in his life. He therefore takes time to think carefully. The superior man exercises caution before he makes a decision, especially, as pictured here, where the right decision is not the obvious one.

Wisdom is the province of the superior man. It is in the making of difficult decisions that wisdom is expressed. The inferior man knows nothing of these matters, and suffers the consequences of his mistakes as if they were natural events rather than brought about by his own unwise decisions made in the past. This is how the inferior man deludes himself that life has no direction or purpose.

Step Six: Hexagram 10 (Sincerity (Honest Intent))

There are certain levels in perception where the superior man is able to see clearly the causes and effects which relate to his personal experiences in life. He knows that at certain times and at certain levels of reality, things are causally related (if he does this, then that will happen). But the superior man also perceives a finer vein to the causal principle – that of quality (if he does this *well*, the outcome will be *fortunate*). Thus he is clear about the value of effort.

When the superior man sets out to do something, he does it well; his work bears the hallmark of quality. For the inferior man, quality is a matter of chance. His work may turn out well, or it may not – he does not make certain of it. Therefore the inferior man can never be certain if his work will bring him good fortune. He quarrels with the superior man about this, but the superior man entertains no such quarrel, for he knows that if a work is done well, it will bring him good fortune.

Synthesis

Your path of Karma is fairly clear. There are few obstacles to achievement and good fortune. As it is your natural disposition to work hard, even when this means self-sacrifice above and beyond the call of duty, you attract beneficial influences throughout your life. All your good fortune will have been justly deserved, but the peculiarity of your Karmic road is that you will often bring good fortune to others when they do not necessarily deserve it. You often make the difference between a positive and negative outcome. In the equation between positive and negative, you tip the balance in favour of the positive. In poetic terms, you are on the side of the angels.

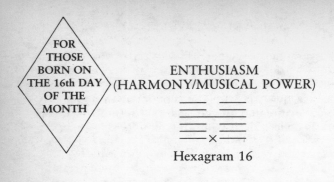

FOR
THOSE
BORN ON
THE 16th DAY
OF THE
MONTH

ENTHUSIASM
(HARMONY/MUSICAL POWER)

Hexagram 16

> *Your Karmic number is 16 (Earth-oriented). The spiritual world is a keenly felt reality for you. You are a truth-seeker and a perfectionist and you are interested mostly in people, literature and any form of artistic expression in which you see the same tendencies. You are happiest in an elevated world of ideals, abstracts. You have an aptitude for manipulating symbols, concepts which have a direct correspondence with 'the truth'. To some extent, you need the security of an emotionally warm relationship, though where this impinges upon your freedom of thought, you are easily irritated. You are often inspired and you should seek work where inspiration is highly valued. Despite all this, you have your feet on the ground, and this suggests that you have a great range of sympathies.*

YOUR ROOT HEXAGRAM: HEXAGRAM 16

Your root hexagram gives the climate or ambience of the six Karmic pictures which are the principal characteristics of your Karmic journey.

The most valuable Karmic lesson to which this hexagram gives utterance is this: follow the line of least resistance. Enshrined in this principle is the idea of *Resonance*: all things have a natural correspondence and are attracted or repelled according to their resident or innate vibration. This is why the hexagram speaks about the force of enthusiasm – which is a high vibration, an expression of genuine joy which comes from the heart and touches all who come into its range. Enthusiasm is contagious, it infects, by its nature, other people. The purest manifestation of 'the high vibration' is music. Everybody knows that music communicates and joins people in a way which is magical. Enthusiasm can be expressed through music; and music inspires positive energy to flow. Music can be the most potent catalyst in the building of bonds between people, and the differences between people can be overcome by 'a common sound'. All this is possible because the fundamental laws of life are explicable in terms of resonance. The laws of resonance are natural laws and they permeate every living thing and every action: 'That is why the celestial bodies do not deviate from their orbits and why all events in nature occur with fixed regularity.' The Laws of Karma are founded on these laws of resonance and because they can be expressed in clearly defined cycles it is possible for man to divine the path of his fate so clearly. If you follow the line of least resistance you are following the law of Karma because it is only another way of defining the expression of Tao in human nature.

Step One: Hexagram 51 (The Arousing/Shock/The Jolt of Fate)

The dynamic relationship between the superior and the inferior men seems to have been forced here by a conspiracy of events into a neutral state. The superior man and the inferior man are locked together in a quantum leap of awareness. The emotion of fear is the inferior man's contribution to the emotional spectrum. Awe and humility are the superior man's contribution.

The inferior man may also feel guilt, that he has come to the end of the road (death), but the superior man feels as though he has been launched into a new world (birth). Such times can be very unsettling because they represent a massive transition from lower to higher. Only the superior man can withstand the force of such times. In a very real sense, what is pictured here is the dynamic of control passing unequivocally into the hands of the superior man. There is an unmistakable feeling that the total situation has in some mystical sense been planned and rigidly defined in order to make the transition successful.

Step Two: Hexagram 54 (Marriage)

Tense and pressured circumstances are pictured here and take their toll on the relationship between the inferior and the superior. The inferior man expects far too much of the superior man at this time and the superior man cannot transform the situation. However, the inferior man remains subservient to the will of the superior man (loyalty) and therefore the relationship does not fall out of harmony.

Step Three: Hexagram 34 (The Leading Initiative)

The superior man is always humble. He never abuses his responsibilities or brings discredit to his position. The inferior man merely revels in his power, and even becomes a tyrant.

Step Four: Hexagram 11 (Peace/Fellowship With Men)

The superior man, despite his material power, is spontaneously attracted to others of similar disposition to himself, but who are not equal in worldly terms.

A wealthy inferior man is never attracted to the superior poor man. When this division persists, there is war between the inferior and superior. Material wealth does not divide superior men – only inferior men.

Step Five: Hexagram 5 (Patience)

The endeavours of the superior man are destined to succeed in the end, but midway in such endeavours, a natural resting place presents itself. The superior man takes advantage of this rest in order to store energy for future challenges. The inferior man, confronted with this break in the progression of events, does not recognise the situation for what it is, and sits around in a state of agitated impatience. Thus when the time to continue endeavours requires replenished energy, the inferior man is exhausted and fails. The superior man is ready to complete the work with success.

Step Six: Hexagram 9 (Limited Persuasion)

A balanced situation pictures mutual understanding between the inferior and the superior man. That situation approaches, but is not fully realised. The inferior man, who sees the end in sight (equilibrium), relaxes, and takes success for granted. The superior man never does this. He continues to be attentive and keeps the objective clearly in mind until it is achieved.

Synthesis

During your Karmic journey you will be confronted with the difficulty of tuning your elevated perception of reality with problems of power and material advantage. But you are well equipped to make these judgments as you have an instinct for harmony and balance. Many situations will provide an opportunity to fine-tune this instinct to great advantage. You have a gift for peace-making; you are a catalyst, a mediator, a translator of abstract into practical.

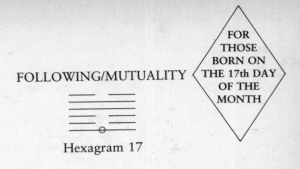

FOLLOWING/MUTUALITY

Hexagram 17

> *Your Karmic number is 17 (Heaven-oriented). You could be a successful businessman as you have a strong entrepreneurial streak, but so long as you confine yourself to main principles rather than the intricate details, you will avoid unnecessary conflicts. You swing constantly like a pendulum between optimism and pessimism and this could be irritating to people close to you. Endowed with a strong will, you should guard against arrogance if you want people to co-operate. Do not be afraid to give your time or your money.*

YOUR ROOT HEXAGRAM: HEXAGRAM 17

Your root hexagram gives the climate or ambience of the six Karmic pictures which are the principal characteristics of your Karmic journey.

One of the fundamental postulates of the *I Ching* is to act *without blame*. You will avoid a great deal of trouble in life if you do not try to win the support or following of others by sneaky or underhand means. This can also mean that while you may see many short-cuts to success, they do not really lead to the goal. You have to realise that if you wish to achieve a true following without attaching blame to yourself and thereby avoid unpleasant comebacks which are only set up by your own actions in the first place, you have to be prepared to work hard and go through all the proper stages. But it is certainly worthwhile: as the *I Ching* says, 'the thought of obtaining a following through adaptation to the demands of the time is a great and significant idea . . . .'

You must also be careful not to work too hard. Take time off to rest.

Step One: Hexagram 45 (The Group)

The superior man knows how to serve the community he has chosen to identify with. He is content that the group functions as a whole and does not necessarily strive to lead it. Nevertheless, the superior man is concerned that the leader of his group or organisation is himself a superior man, capable and able, with a vocation for the task. The superior man who has doubts about leadership expresses them to the leader.

The inferior man gossips behind the leader's back and complains to other members of the group. The inferior man's actions are divisive and seek to upset harmonious relationships through insensitive criticism. The superior man is constructive in his criticism and he directs it at the appropriate person at the appropriate time and place.

Step Two: Hexagram 47 (Depression)

This is a picture of a pressured situation. When the superior man is under pressure of any kind, he takes the view that the situation offers him the opportunity for self-improvement. The superior man is grateful for the things he has and for the help he is offered. The inferior man is envious. He looks to those things that he does not have; nothing suffices for him; he is always desirous of more. It is this condition which has produced the pressure of the situation, the inner tension. The superior man releases this tension by adopting an attitude of gratitude and this leads to an attitude of patience. Thus the superior man at these times is not concerned with looking far into the future, but making good of what he has today. The inferior man is never satisfied and sets up a chain reaction of dissatisfaction by his own ingratitude. If this cycle is allowed to continue, it will have the effect of increasing the pressure on the inferior man until it is so great that he can make no further progress. The inferior man is thus brought to a stop.

When the inferior man has lost control over volition, the superior man takes over.

Step Three: Hexagram 28 (Under Pressure)

This Karmic picture depicts the logical development of the last step. Here the inferior man has allowed the spiral of pressure brought about by conceit, ingratitude, persistent and inappropriate force, to land him in a predicament where he can neither go forwards nor back. The inferior man has now come to a stop.

If the inferior man tries to make any kind of impression on his situation, he will merely sink deeper into the quagmire. In such a situation the superior man attempts to do nothing; he waits; he keeps perfectly still. The superior man knows that the natural cycle of events will bring about a change in his relative position in the world and a way out (a tension release) will eventually present itself. The superior man knows he cannot force this new light to appear — it will come when it will. He therefore waits for it. He has no choice.

Step Four: Hexagram 48 (The Well)

The superior man does not wait for the force of circumstance to compel him into a period of self-examination. He plans for these periods and takes full advantage of a period of inactivity in order to put his thoughts into clear perspective again. He knows that only from a position of spiritual clarity can he be really effective in the world and bring order into events.

There is no quarrel between the superior man and the inferior man in this Karmic picture. Thus the superior man is able to advance in his spiritual development without outside distractions.

Step Five: Hexagram 46 (Beginning of Ascent)

The superior man is consistent in his efforts even at the precarious moment when the work is almost completed. The inferior man will look back over the considerable achievements of the superior man after a period of sustained successful activity, but this looking back is not careful reflection and is not truly a part of the work of completion, but is more an act of gloating or self-congratulation. The superior man only looks at past work in order to learn best how to complete it. He looks for patterns, reflects on the meaning of the past in order to work out his future strategy – in this case, to complete the work he has begun. He will use such a pause to steady his hand for the final act and to ensure that every detail is as it should be.

If there is going to be a mistake, the inferior man will make it now.

Step Six: Hexagram 18 (Work on What Has Been Spoiled)

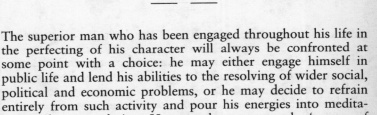

The superior man who has been engaged throughout his life in the perfecting of his character will always be confronted at some point with a choice: he may either engage himself in public life and lend his abilities to the resolving of wider social, political and economic problems, or he may decide to refrain entirely from such activity and pour his energies into meditation and contemplation. He may choose not to be 'a man of action'. However, both paths lead to the same spiritual goal for the superior man. How the superior man chooses is a personal matter.

The point here is that the superior man who chooses to retreat from the world does not do so in order to provide a comfortable stance from which he may jeer, sneer, and indulge in over-critical attitudes towards those who are engaged in the world of action. In those circumstances, only the inferior man indulges in underlining the faults of others as his principal activity. The superior man never abuses his comforts. He is either constructive or he is silent. He turns away from the world only to develop himself and not to throw mud from the sidelines.

Synthesis

Your Karmic road provides immense scope for action and achievement. Only a tendency to self-glorification and selfishness impedes you. The weak points on your road are the places where you come to natural stops, or are forced by negative circumstances to halt. Knowing what to do in these moments of inactivity is the key to your success or your undoing.

FOR
THOSE
BORN ON
THE 18th DAY
OF THE
MONTH

WORK ON WHAT HAS BEEN SPOILED

Hexagram 18

> *Your Karmic number is 18 (Earth-oriented). You are a kind person, and people are naturally attracted to you. People find you intellectually stimulating company, and you make a good friend. Though not necessarily creative yourself, you have a love of art and music and you admire creative people. However, you do have certain negative qualities. You can be lazy, dogmatic, even narrow-minded. You sometimes have difficulty seeing things through other people's eyes, and this is your blind spot, because you think you can do this very well, and often regard yourself as a good judge of ability. True excellence in people often slips through your fingers because you are too prejudiced to see it. Travel will broaden your horizons, and it should figure prominently in your life. Don't let people take your kind nature for granted.*

YOUR ROOT HEXAGRAM: HEXAGRAM 18

Your root hexagram gives the climate or ambience of the six Karmic pictures which are the principal characteristics of your Karmic journey.

Despite your obvious charisma and energy for action which will characterise your life, you will not enter into the truly productive phase of your travels until you have made a conscious commitment that nothing can be achieved without consistent hard work. You have a highly pronounced lazy streak which causes you to delude yourself into thinking that 'tomorrow will do'. At some point in your life you will recognise that a couple of years have gone by during which you have wanted to achieve a great deal, but have actually achieved nothing. If you take the lesson to heart then, you will decide to really apply yourself and then anything can happen, for you have great energy and a lot going for you. Your natural gifts for winning the co-operation of others, for inspiration and insight into the needs of people and your particular fascination for trends in society and your curious ability to respond to those trends in an original and creative way will bring you great reward. The essence of your success will be consistency in the application of effort and this should come with maturity.

The more highly developed individual with this Karmic root will have the power to fill others with enthusiasm and to regenerate their spirit and interest in ideas and work. You have no trouble in sniffing out corrupting influences which can sabotage projects and you have an uncanny habit of coming up with exactly the right solution. If, during your youth, you have developed a strong concentration, you could make a lot of difference to the condition of society and the way people in large numbers view themselves. This is the way the leader in you manifests itself. However, to get to this point, you must learn consistency and resilience in the face of setbacks. Avoid the 'Who cares?' attitude, for it is just self-delusion.

Step One: Hexagram 26 (Held in Check)

When the time comes for the superior man to act after a long period of waiting, he is able to unleash such a force of creative energy that immense achievements may be realised. The superior man is not in any conflict with the inferior man.

Step Two: Hexagram 22 (Art)

The superior man and the inferior man are very far apart here. The superior man rests. He partakes of pleasures, he may enjoy the good things in life. The inferior man is idle. He indulges himself to excess in superficial pleasures. He plays the rake; he is vain, clubbish, elitist. He is under the powerful but utterly false apprehension that he is the soul of the superior man. The inferior man is, here, so far away from the ways of the superior man, that he can be said to be almost totally blind. The inferior man here is so intoxicated with his vanity that he does not know he is vain or intoxicated. If the situation is allowed to go to extremes, the inferior man could destroy himself without even realising that he was in danger. The superior man never allows his awareness to shrink.

Step Three: Hexagram 27 (Health)

This Karmic frame is an extension of the previous step. Here the inferior man aggravates his inferiority by harming his body, through over-indulgence in drugs or alcohol. The inferior man may become dependent upon substances which diminish awareness substantially. The superior man avoids addiction to any such substance. He never allows himself to become dependent upon anything which will cause his awareness to shrink. The superior man maintains his body in the best possible condition: he does nothing wilfully to damage it.

Step Four: Hexagram 21 (Decisive Action)

The Karmic picture here is of a difficult situation. The superior man regards this as a challenge. He never approaches a challenge with an attitude of over-confidence. He never underestimates his opponent under any circumstances. The situation demands of the superior man sustained concentration.

If the inferior man's concentration slips even for a moment, he will lose.

Step Five: Hexagram 25 (Innocence)

The superior man takes responsibility for any mistakes he makes, but any harm which comes to him which is not of his own making, or his own fault, is not his responsibility. That is to say, he must not seek to redress the balance or take any kind of revenge, as this would only force circumstances even further out of harmony. A very high idea is being postulated here: that of cosmic justice.

The principle of the Tao is that everything is in a natural state of harmony. Whenever this harmony is disturbed by an outside force it will naturally right itself and harmony will be restored once again. But if an individual takes it upon himself to redress wrongs or try to force an unnatural balance in events, he will only perpetuate the imbalance. Thus we can see that revenge, in all its forms, falls into this category and creates a spiral of chaos which can perpetuate through centuries. Thus the natural balance and force of the Tao is inhibited.

The superior man knows that whatever is his can never be

taken away. In the natural balance, it is always connected to him. The inferior man in a state of discord is susceptible to the illusion that he can restore the balance of the Tao as he experiences it, but in so thinking, he acts against the Tao and therefore perpetuates the imbalance. The more he persists in this the longer he is separated from what is his. If the inferior man would only be still in the face of conflict, he would come to understand this immutable law of change, and the way of the superior man.

Step Six: Hexagram 17 (Mutuality)

Here the inferior man and the superior man are in mutual and congenial dialogue. Their purpose is to work together to produce something of benefit for others. Thus the relationship of inferior to superior is dignified and is held in high esteem by other superior people. This frame pictures the world of action and the world of the spirit acting in harmony.

Synthesis

Your Karmic road is not an easy one. Only when you are in possession of all your faculties and where you have learned to develop your concentration will you stand a chance against the obstacles you will come up against. Negative and positive in your Karmic road are well-matched opponents, and for the positive to win in the end you must avoid anything and everything that can muddle your head.

THE OPEN DOOR

Hexagram 19

> *Your Karmic number is 19 (Heaven-oriented). You could be described as an adventurer. You sail very close to the wind in your personal affairs. You are keenly interested in a wide variety of ideas, but you find it difficult to settle your views or be consistent in your actions. You may find it difficult to keep promises. You have tremendous mental and physical stamina, however, and you can be startlingly original and resourceful, and this will enable you to sail through many storms. If you want a quieter life, you must deliberately sail into calmer waters. In order to offset the dangers attendant on your personality, you should cultivate relationships with people who on the one hand accept you for what you are and don't seek to change that, while on the other hand can anchor you when you take risks. You have in your nature extremes of hardness and softness which co-exist.*

YOUR ROOT HEXAGRAM: HEXAGRAM 19

Your root hexagram gives the climate or ambience of the six Karmic pictures which are the principal characteristics of your Karmic journey.

This hexagram is called 'Approach' or 'The Open Door'. In the *I Ching* this signifies a person who has no difficulty in successfully communicating his ideas to people. People find you interesting and are willing to entertain your opinions. Although you may not be employed as a professional teacher in a conventional sense, what you do amounts to helping people understand things. This is a natural characteristic. The law of the Tao is that if one wishes to be successful, one must take the line of least resistance. Thus, if your talents lead you in a particular direction, don't fight it. The idea of timing is also important, namely, it is useless to try and make people understand things unless you perceive that the conditions are ready for it. People never really learn anything unless they want to and it is impossible to force people to understand anything. Learning is always a personal responsibility and as long as you understand that, you will not waste energy planting seeds in infertile soil. A preliminary step to teaching, therefore, is the cultivation of interest, and this is always a matter of the right time. The more developed you become, the wider your sympathies and the greater your aptitude to open the windows of the mind for others. This is auspicious. You will encounter many opportunities on your path to exercise your benevolent instincts and for you this is the road to self-fulfilment.

Step One: Hexagram 7 (Challenge)

The Karmic picture here is of the superior man in preparation to meet a challenge. The word 'challenge' has many connotations; it can mean a sporting challenge, for example, or a challenge which involves more important consequences for the superior man. In the latter event, the superior man first examines his motives for entering into any kind of challenge. The inferior man is not concerned with examining his motives. Revenge may be a suitable motive for entering into a challenge for the inferior man, for example, whereas for the superior man, revenge is never a motive. Having examined his motives, the superior man in his preparations is careful to see that he is well-equipped — in terms of the forces at his disposal — adequately to meet the challenge. If his forces are comprised of people, then he makes sure of the competence of each person.

He is thorough and meticulous in every detail with regard to his own forces.

Step Two: Hexagram 2 (The Receptive)

The situation pictured here is of a time when the superior man is prudent not to draw attention to himself. He is therefore able to work without intimidation from the inferior man or from anyone else. He does not seek acclaim, recognition or promotion for any of the work he is doing even if it is forthcoming. He lets his work stand on its own. This preserves his freedom and his personal momentum. The inferior man is keen to draw attention to himself. He works for fame. His work suffers if he does not gain recognition. His motives find their root in the glorification of his personality.

In such times the inferior man attracts to himself those who will harm the work of the superior man. Thus the superior man withdraws from the inferior man into quiet seclusion and does not allow himself to be tempted away from the actual achievements.

Step Three: Hexagram 15 (Modesty)

The situation pictured here is of a superior man whose work has been recognised and for which he has been rewarded. But for the superior man, these are ephemeral considerations. Co-operation and help, which further the work, are what impress the superior man and for these things he shows gratitude.

Step Four: Hexagram 62 (Over-Enthusiasm)

The superior man considers time spent in contemplation of a particular plan of action to be of greater value than the action itself. The thoughts of the superior man may have an effect upon a particular situation even though he is not overtly active in it. Because of this, the superior man is very cautious not to force himself upon a situation in case in so doing he causes effects that are undesirable. In such a situation he prefers not to act at all but to wait in readiness.

Step Five: Hexagram 31 (Natural Attraction)

In order that the superior man may influence the inferior man, he must be, in a very special sense, receptive to the influence of the inferior man. In this way he understands the inferior man's feelings. If the superior man were not open to influence he could not hope to have any influence himself.

The inferior man enforces his view on others and this arouses resentment and rejection and thus his view has no influence.

Step Six: Hexagram 33 (Retreat)

The superior man recognises when the cycle of a relationship with another has come to a natural end. At such times it is right for him to take his leave. It is not always possible for him to do this as the person he is leaving may be reluctant to see him go, and the situation may therefore be embarrassing. However, as in this case, he is able to leave while the relationship is at its strongest: in a condition of mutual trust. The superior man always prefers this outcome, and thus his leavetaking is in good spirit.

For the inferior man, it is a matter of no consequence that the feelings of the other party are important.

Synthesis

As long as you concentrate on the quality of the work that you do, and do not allow yourself to be distracted by rewards, such as fame or glory, you will be able to retain your freedom to work more or less on your own terms, and therefore you will avoid personal conflicts.

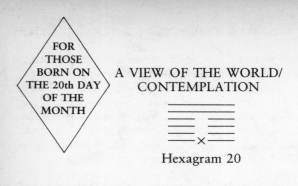

FOR THOSE BORN ON THE 20th DAY OF THE MONTH

A VIEW OF THE WORLD/ CONTEMPLATION

Hexagram 20

Your Karmic number is 20 (Earth-oriented). A harmonious environment is a vital prerequisite for your happiness and success. You like to work with people you know well and have come to trust. Out of this comes your confidence to deal with strangers with poise. You are a person of many abilities which range from the creative arts to highly practical matters. You like to see things stand completed and perfected, as you are a perfectionist yourself. You like neat, clean edges — you could be anything from a mathematician to a dress designer. This is not the same as being a stickler for details in a superficial way. Your concern is to understand the structure in detail in order to refine the expression of the content. The principle applies to any exact science — this might include architecture, mathematics, music, language et al.

YOUR ROOT HEXAGRAM: HEXAGRAM 20

Your root hexagram gives the climate or ambience of the six Karmic pictures which are the principal characteristics of your Karmic journey.

You have a natural interest in and fascination for understanding how things work. You have an innate propensity for serious study and the gift of your Karmic path in life is that you are able to think deeply about ideas. Thus you are very rarely disoriented as you tend to appreciate the surrounding landscape in relation to your own position. Whether or not this aptitude

124

expresses itself in your desire to get the bird's eye view of ideas or of literally climbing up to the tops of mountains and looking around you, it is still an aptitude for getting a lot of ideas into perspective and for penetrating mysteries. In a very real sense, you are a traveller. Whether you are travelling through the landscape of abstract ideas, or backwards through time in the study of history, or literally travelling in foreign parts, this is how you will best express the will of your spirit.

It may well be that as you come to understand more and more the mysteries of life, so you will curiously radiate a kind of wisdom which has an unmistakably positive effect on all those who come into contact with you. There is something pure about this Karmic road which may have the effect, despite your wider view, of making you something of a purist. As long as you recognise this trait in your character and cultivate your aptitude for deeper understanding, you will find many of the obstacles in the normal round of events comparatively superficial. You are not an easy person to fool. It may be worthwhile to record your insights in some form. Although for you it may not be important to do so (you may feel that it is enough for you to understand), there is an unmistakable value in making your insights available to others.

Step One: Hexagram 42 (Spiritual Wealth)

There is no conflict between the superior and inferior man, but the superior man has been working unassisted. Now he receives all the help he requires from another superior man. When two superior men join together in a common task, they are able to produce remarkable results. This is indeed auspicious as the work has every chance of enduring.

Step Two: Hexagram 61 (Inner Truth)

The situation pictured here has a far-reaching importance because it embraces one of the least understood laws of the superior way and the superior man: there is no situation possible on the earth which does not in itself hold the seed of a superior response. This means that the superior man is able to act with absolute consistency in any situation without compromising his superiority. Indeed, it is the purpose of this book to demonstrate and testify to that fact. The *I Ching* posits, through the six lines or Karmic pictures of each of the sixty-four hexagrams, all the possible human dynamics which alone and in combination give rise to the spectrum of reality in the visible and invisible world. In none of those situations, singly or in combination, is the superior man without a superior position. Thus, it should be plain that the superior way links up all those who embody it, no matter where on the earth they are, and those who adhere to the superior way in their own nature are empathically and resonantly in touch with all those who also embody the superior way. In itself this is a far-reaching idea, about which we are certain to hear more in the future. Unlike other forces which connect people up in the world (religions and ideologies, for example) the veracity of the superior way is not dependent upon belief but may embrace many religions and ideologies in an incidental way.

This is the idea which the superior man understands. However he may have expressed it to himself, and in whatever language, he perceives the interconnectedness of himself and the superior way — or Tao. Understanding this single concept enables the superior man to comprehend and distinguish the ways of the inferior man. In that crucial distinction lie the seeds of all understanding.

Step Three: Hexagram 9 (Limited Persuasion)

Here are pictured the effects of the influence the inferior man has tried to bring to bear, brashly and confidently expecting to be met with agreement. He has misunderstood and misgauged the extent and power of his own influence because he has underestimated the complexity of the situation which he wishes to change. Disagreements and bickering result.

The superior man refrains from attempting to influence a situation without a more detailed understanding. It is prudent for the superior man to calculate the effect of any change that he may be instrumental in bringing about in the affairs of others.

Step Four: Hexagram 1 (The Creative)

The situation pictured here is that the superior man is faced with a choice as to how he expresses his creative contribution to life. He knows that the choice is a personal one and depends upon his personality. He also knows that in terms of the effects he will have, either option will create the opportunity to make an equal contribution. One is not preferred over the other because it is more or less important in some social sense. He may either enter the public arena and work among people, or he may prefer to work behind the scenes in private. There is no conflict with the inferior man.

Step Five: Hexagram 14 (Wealth)

Even the most kindhearted and well-disposed of superior men refrains from bestowing his benevolence upon those who do not need it. The inferior man does not show such awareness even in acts of kindness and is easily upset if his kindness is refused for reasons he may not understand.

Step Six: Hexagram 34 (Leading Initiative)

Here the inferior man wishes to make progress but he cannot do so as he has become entangled in the very thing he is pushing against. The situation is further complicated by the fact that he has become so entangled that he cannot retreat either. Thus any movement the inferior man makes either forward or back creates further entanglement. If he realises what is happening, he will keep still. Without any further effort on the inferior man's part, the predicament in which he finds himself will be naturally resolved, and he will be freed from the entanglement.

The same would hold true of the superior man, except that he does not oppose his fate and thus does not needlessly complicate issues which are already complex enough. He does everything he can to simplify them.

Synthesis

Your Karmic road leads you into the high country and enables you to see the surrounding landscape in all its numerous patterns and complexities and diversity. Thus you are able to find your place in the scheme of things. If you can hold on to the key ideas you will be able to orient yourself successfully through any situation in which you find yourself. You have the benefit of having achieved a panoramic view. This is an advantage not given to everyone. It is likely that you will intersect on your Karmic journey with others who would benefit from your wider view of the world.

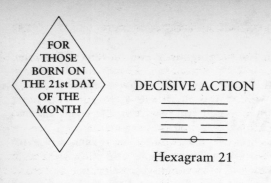

FOR
THOSE
BORN ON
THE 21st DAY
OF THE
MONTH

DECISIVE ACTION

Hexagram 21

> *Your Karmic number is 21 (Heaven-oriented). You need a balance between a calm and pleasant environment, stable personal relationships and creative challenge in which to express your individualism. You must be aware that if you do not focus your energies and consciously limit yourself to specific areas of interest, you run the risk of not achieving anything. Since you prefer to relax while doing something, you should take care to balance your surplus energy between mental and physical activity. You are socially popular.*

YOUR ROOT HEXAGRAM: HEXAGRAM 21

Your root hexagram gives the climate or ambience of the six Karmic pictures which are the principal characteristics of your Karmic journey.

At some point in your life, you are going to come into contact with that system of rules and regulations which defines most fields of action in society: the legal system. The essence of your contact lies in your ability to have a clear view of the idea of justice. Thus if you encounter legal obstacles, the important thing is to get the whole situation into a crystal clear perspective before you start. This avoids delay. There will be a tendency to let the making of legal decisions drag on interminably but if this is allowed to happen the whole point of justice (where the problem or the offence or the matter for resolution must bear some close proximity to the final decision) is lost. The law, in order to be effective, must administer justice swiftly, otherwise it has no poignancy and no effect. The same applies to the relationship between an offence and the time it takes to bring the matter to trial and the quality of the punishment. The Taoist view is that there is absolutely no point in criminal law suits in meting out punishments which have no real effect in changing the heart of the offender. Long years of imprisonment are no answer, for example, as after a very short time the relationship between the offence and the punishment loses its clarity and therefore its poignancy, relevance and effect in the mind of the offender, and without poignancy, relevance and effect, how do you define justice? The execution of justice must not be a lengthy, drawn-out affair.

The second observation to be made is that if individuals take the law into their own hands, as a general rule, the fabric of society will be destroyed in a very short space of time. Thus no exceptions to the rule can be tolerated. If these two points are borne in mind and you are quick to resolve legal issues, such obstacles need not inhibit your journey through life more than they ought. The matter is over and done with and you can go on your way. Unnaturally prolonging tension does nobody any good because it destroys the natural balance. This is why the hexagram is called 'Biting through'. One bites through these obstacles.

Step One: Hexagram 35 (Progress)

The superior man perseveres in his positive actions and positive intentions even under the difficult circumstances where others cannot keep up with him or do not have sufficient energy to co-operate. Under such circumstances the inferior man is easily aroused to anger and will halt his progress in order to forcefully change the situation to his own advantage.

Step Two: Hexagram 64 (Before Completion)

The Karmic picture here is of the superior man engaged in creative projects who has now reached a natural lull. In order to overcome the danger of losing energy, he maintains his interest in his objectives by studying carefully the work he has achieved so far. That is to say, he keeps himself positively engaged in the work although he cannot at this time make any progress.

The inferior man, when stopped in this way, quickly loses interest; he makes no attempt to sustain his interest in order to bring the work to fruition and so it is uncertain whether the inferior man's work will ever be completed.

Step Three: Hexagram 50 (Valuable Work)

The superior man, even when he receives no help, approval, co-operation and recognition for his work, and is thereby impeded in continuing his work through a lack of resources, does not take the matter personally. He continues to work hard and does not lose heart. Such consistent rejection is enough to make the inferior man lose heart so that he abandons the work altogether. The superior man continues the work for its own sake, because it is intrinsically valuable to him.

The situation for the superior man therefore sets up a resonance which will eventually bring the work into the light of day.

Step Four: Hexagram 18 (Work on What Has Been Spoiled)

Where the superior man detects mistakes, faults or problems in any situation or in work in which he is engaged, he takes action to cure the problem at its roots as quickly as possible. He knows that fundamental faults will only threaten the ultimate results and later destabilise the work at a critical moment. The inferior man deludes himself into thinking that all is well, and does nothing, and therefore suffers the consequences of his neglect when at some later point the overall work, structure, or relationship is undermined.

Step Five: Hexagram 57 (The Impressionable)

The superior man understands a vital principle of the Tao: that the quality of the end product is inextricably linked to the quality of its beginnings. Here the Karmic picture represents a period after many difficulties have been overcome, and a clear Karmic road lies ahead. The superior man takes thought to ensure that he makes his new beginning sound and strong in order to ensure that the outcome of his efforts will bear good fruit for the future. Thus he avoids mistakes.

Step Six: Hexagram 48 (The Well)

Here the superior man has triumphed in his work and makes available to all peoples indiscriminately the fruits of his work. They may take according to their needs without ever exhausting the facility. Such a state of affairs is an auspicious blessing which has the power to endure in time. The superior man has here achieved the greatest possible contribution to mankind and his work and life stand as an example.

Synthesis

There are many heartrending difficulties on your Karmic path but the possibility of bringing about a lasting achievement never deserts your life. If you persevere despite all the rejections and rebuffs (much more difficult than it sounds) you must ultimately overcome. Many people are defeated by this Karmic road because they do not persevere.

GRACE
(AESTHETICS/ART/SYMMETRY)

FOR
THOSE
BORN ON
THE 22nd DAY
OF THE
MONTH

Hexagram 22

> *Your Karmic number is 22 (Earth-oriented). You will feel a strong sense of destiny throughout your life. You may be conscious of having been set a particular task or job to do. Undoubtedly you have the propensity for great achievement and it may be your fate to give shape or voice to an important set of values which will have significance for mankind as a whole. If you yourself are not the architect of these values, you may be their mouthpiece, one of their champions. You, or the work, or both, at the most auspicious moment and for good or ill, must receive public recognition. Thus, because of the power invested in this Karmic journey, you have no choice but to maintain the very highest moral standards. Failure to do so could have catastrophic consequences. But it must be said that if you fulfil your destiny according to its highest potential, mankind could be blessed through you and your work endure through time.*

YOUR ROOT HEXAGRAM: HEXAGRAM 22

Your root hexagram gives the climate or ambience of the six Karmic pictures which are the principal characteristics of your Karmic journey.

Very early in life you are going to grasp the idea that you have been born with a lucky streak. But in the Tao there is no such thing as luck; the Fates of men are subject to immutable laws and you have been born onto a Karmic road which gives you not only the opportunity for great achievement, but also the energy to make those achievements real. The Karmic frames which follow describe the principal challenges which you must be aware of if you are going to fulfil your remarkable and god-given potential. For people born onto this Karmic road, it would be nothing short of a tragedy if the brightness of their achievements did not veritably light up the sky.

Although the hexagram is called 'Grace', which in terms of the above speaks for itself, its other meaning is the representation of potential in some creative form – hence art, aesthetics, the appreciation of the structured expression of life. How you express yourself in life is not prescribed, whether it be in the theatre, as a painter, as a musician, an engineer, inventor, sculptor, architect, even as a politician, you are going to bring to *whatever* you do a certain magical energy. You are going to push back the frontiers in your chosen field. If you do it well, your work will have duration through time. The added dimension to all this is that you can do it all in such a pleasing way. Therein lies the gift – people are going to like you for what you do.

Step One: Hexagram 52 (Learning to Relax)

The superior man who is marked out by destiny to pursue a particular course of action will have an early intuition in his life which will have great impact on his thinking. Everything that follows depends upon whether the superior man is able to lock on to his destiny and never allow himself to be distracted from his ultimate purpose. While at times he may be confronted by apparently insuperable obstacles which force him either to wait or go round them, he can never be distracted from keeping to his path. The superior man here is impossible to distract. His perception of his destiny becomes increasingly crystal clear.

Step Two: Hexagram 18 (Work on What Has Been Spoiled)

Despite the strong guiding light of the superior man in this Karmic frame, he must nevertheless show tolerance and forbearance when he confronts difficulties brought about by others, even unknowingly. Here, the problems which may beset the superior man are brought about by his mother, or the mother principle in his life. The inferior man may wish to respond in order to put things right in an over-energetic and over-enthusiastic manner. The superior man adopts an attitude of broad-minded tolerance.

Step Three: Hexagram 4 (Inexperience of the Young/The Student)

The superior man, especially where his destiny has a powerful current, allows his imagination to wander into strange and wonderful places, but this is not always relevant and helpful in the fulfilment of his destiny. For him, his imagination is central to his path in life, but only if it is properly directed. Only the inferior man allows his imagination to lead him astray. The superior man controls his imagination. He directs it, shapes it, gives it form, and in this he is particularly talented.

If imagination of this magnitude is not controlled and shaped, the inferior man can lose his way in the world.

Step Four: Hexagram 64 (Before Completion)

Here is the place of transition. The inferior man and the superior man are opposed and in conflict. The superior man is stronger than the inferior man but he must fight with all his energy the temptations and distractions deliberately thrown in his path by the inferior man. If the inferior man overcomes, the superior man will never realise the achievements which were his birthright. Therefore the superior man has everything to fight for. In a very real sense he is fighting for his own destiny, his right to achieve the things he was born for. In crystal clear terms, what is being decided in this conflict is who will rule this life, the inferior man or the superior man. The inferior man cannot rule anybody. All he can do is prevent the superior man from ruling him. Thus the superior man must rule the inferior man if he is to rule his destiny. In still plainer terms, we are talking of will-power and self-control.

In the whole Karmic journey, this conflict is inevitable. This is the acid test.

Step Five: Hexagram 6 (Conflict/Deadlock)

The role of the superior man in this Karmic picture is to be the arbiter in a dispute in which he is not personally involved. The duties of the superior man in such a position require him to be utterly fair, impartial, unprejudiced. He must clearly see the merits of the relative positions of both sides. They in turn must be willing to abide by the final decision. Only the superior man can be an arbiter in any dispute. The inferior man does not have the necessary qualities.

Step Six: Hexagram 47 (Depression)

The picture here is of the superior man who is presented with an opportunity to show his colours, but because he does not fully understand the nature of his destiny, his natural impulsion is to procrastinate. He feels inhibited and does not wish to make an impression. Therefore the picture is one of indecision. However, because this is an important juncture in the superior man's destiny, he receives an insight, a flash of illumination which enables him to gain a clear and correct perspective. In this way, all inhibition is swept away and the decision is made. Once the superior man has decided, there is no looking back. Here the superior man is consciously acknowledging his destiny. For him this is the most important moment of his life. All things flow from it.

Synthesis

Once you know that your life is guided by a powerful destiny, and you have developed the strength to look it in the eye and live up to its challenges, you will be able to fulfil your promise of achievement. Not until you have done this will you achieve anything.

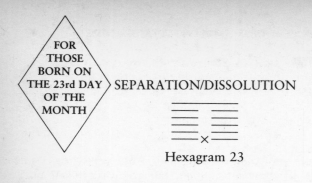

FOR THOSE BORN ON THE 23rd DAY OF THE MONTH

SEPARATION/DISSOLUTION

Hexagram 23

> *Your Karmic number is 23 (Heaven-oriented). You have the versatility to turn your hand to anything that you choose to do. The distinctions between practical and abstract hold no special problem for you. You are at home in both. You have keen powers of concentration and the ability to see things whole. You are a very difficult person to deceive as you have a remarkable facility for seeing through people, but this ability also extends into your ability to see hidden problems or thoughts which may escape the attention of other people. Being quick-minded, you are naturally adaptable. You can feel at home in a variety of different situations. Pride may be a problem and you may defend your independence fiercely.*

YOUR ROOT HEXAGRAM: HEXAGRAM 23

Your root hexagram gives the climate or ambience of the six Karmic pictures which are the principal characteristics of your Karmic journey.

The secret of your success is in how you cope with adversity. When you meet adversity in life, you may be prompted to strike back, respond with violence, take revenge. If you are going to make mistakes in life they will be in this respect. The hardest thing to do is to cope with adversity through being exactly the opposite of antagonistic and vengeful, that is by being quiet and still. If you understand that the reason you may be aroused to anger by unforeseen obstacles coming unasked for into your life is that you feel that life is being unduly unfair to you; you recognise that the difficulties were not of your own making, so it may seem natural that you want to remove them forcefully. If you can avoid this response, understandable though it is, and recognise that the obstacle will pass of its own accord without any intervention from you (the strength to be still) you will save yourself a lot of heartache and needless entanglement. This is the secret of a clear road.

You also have a tendency to look back in anger and this can be a serious impediment to your innate generosity. In old age, you might seek to take revenge on society by being something of a miser, but this is just an extension of exactly the same principle of responding antagonistically to obstacles. You can only break this wheel of Karma by making a conscious decision not to react. Alignment with the Tao here is *not-doing*.

Step One: Hexagram 27 (Health)

Among the most unattractive characteristics of the inferior man is his tendency to compare his own station in life with those whom he regards as more fortunate than himself. The inferior man feels envy. He is jealous not only of the possessions of other people but also of their talents and qualities. This brings him into conflict with the superior man who uses what he has to make himself independent and self-sufficient. The superior man does not regard his possessions and his qualities as a basis for generating conflicts with other people.

Step Two: Hexagram 41 (External Poverty)

The superior man who wishes to be of assistance to other superior men does not attempt to give more than he actually has to give. That is to say, he does not exhaust himself as this would only decrease his ability to be of any use, and his actions would therefore have no duration. The superior man spares himself and knows that this is dignity. The inferior man spends himself all too quickly, and because his actions have no duration, he quickly brings discredit upon himself.

Step Three: Hexagram 26 (Held in Check)

The Karmic picture is one of the superior man who has been held in restraint by external forces over which he has no control. But this restraint is intentional as it is not yet time for the superior man to release his energies in a constructive way. If the restraint were not present, the inferior man, having no self-control, would prematurely expend what energies he has to no great effect. Thus, for the superior man, he regards the restraint as a period in which he can store energy for future action so that he is able to acquit himself well in the field of action. The inferior man regards this time as a tiresome limitation, but because the constraints are so strong, he cannot, even if he wants to, waste his energy. Thus superior and inferior are yoked together tightly.

Once the dynamic between the superior and inferior in the way pictured here is clearly understood, then the idea of the release of restraint can be fully appreciated for what it is, as this is what happens next.

Step Four: Hexagram 14 (Wealth)

The Karmic picture is of material gain, but as before, there is the strong tendency of the inferior man to dominate the attitude towards wealth. He will compare the magnitude of his wealth and possessions with the wealth and possessions of others. As a mental process, this creates an unlimited spiral of confusion as all the relative states now conspire to lose the inferior man. The superior man never regards wealth in this way and therefore retains his clarity at all costs. He is aware of the transient and ephemeral nature of the material world and does not allow himself to be implicated in its nefarious designs. He sees it for what it is and makes use of it accordingly. He sees no cause for pride in the accumulation of possessions for its own sake – only the inferior man is concerned with such things.

Step Five: Hexagram 1 (The Creative)

There is no conflict between the superior man and the inferior man. The superior man realises the pinnacle of creative achievement and stands as a beacon of light to guide others. Where the superior man is able to bring his powers to perfect expression in himself, he sets a standard of excellence which endures through time. In such examples, mankind is blessed.

Step Six: Hexagram 43 (The Beginning of Ascent)

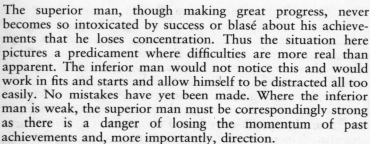

The superior man, though making great progress, never becomes so intoxicated by success or blasé about his achievements that he loses concentration. Thus the situation here pictures a predicament where difficulties are more real than apparent. The inferior man would not notice this and would work in fits and starts and allow himself to be distracted all too easily. No mistakes have yet been made. Where the inferior man is weak, the superior man must be correspondingly strong as there is a danger of losing the momentum of past achievements and, more importantly, direction.

The inferior man is liable to exhaust himself in chasing mirages. The superior man trusts his compass.

Synthesis

Because you have many possibilities in life, but only one Karmic road, you will always be presented with difficult choices. But the difficulty lies in not understanding your true direction. The so-called alternative directions which you perceive so clearly are chimeras. Thus, when you see at some point in your life the clear road of achievement, note it carefully so that at some later point, when you are thrown into indecision, you can refer to it and remember. Through this, you will overcome your most serious obstacle, as the rest is clear.

Hexagram 24

Your Karmic number is 24 (Earth-oriented). You are zealous and single-minded and, as a rule, you are fearless, too. You easily accept the need to work hard, but you are not above imposing your views on other people if you feel that they are not listening. You are perhaps over-energetic, but you compensate for this by being highly motivated. You tend to direct most of your energy into improving conditions and taking an interest in domestic and social affairs. You like to organise other people and in a teaching environment many of your abilities would shine.

YOUR ROOT HEXAGRAM: HEXAGRAM 24

This is the number of the Great Transition, or Turning Point. It means change on a grand scale; the complete transformation of the quality of experience. It is also a reference to a change in the atmosphere and ambience of the time. One experiences such a time as a change from sluggish to smooth, from twilight to light, from heavy hearted to light hearted. The time is about 'upswing', when things start to come together and the bits start to fall into place, but, and here's the crucial part, the change comes of itself, it comes naturally, not as a forced event.

The lesson here for Karma is to refrain from interfering in natural processes. This is not so much impatience, but the inability to recognise patterns of events over time. Unlike Root 5 where patience must be learned, or Root 18 where special effort must be made if progress is to be made, here the change is seen like a giant turning wheel. The individual is powerless to make it go faster or slower. One merely rides it. The quality of the experience of Transformation to Light can be maximised by relaxing into it.

The pressures of life withdraw. The new cycle of life manifests itself out of a long accumulation of past tendencies.

Step One: Hexagram 2 (The Receptive)

The superior man shows foresight in the natural round of events. He recognises the order implicit in the seasons of the year. Although Spring is the time of new flowering and growth, the superior man knows that part of that same cycle is the period of decay and death. He therefore takes precautions, recognising the yin within the yang and the yang within the yin, preparing especially for the time of decay, in order to avoid being caught out by it. The inferior man pays no heed to the seasons and the natural cycles of life, particularly where these cycles are heavily disguised by artificial environments such as in a city. Each season bears its own characteristics regardless of how he might like to insulate himself from it.

Step Two: Hexagram 7 (Challenge)

The Karmic picture is of the superior man in the role of a leader of a challenging force. When the superior man leads, he leads from the front and not the rear. He guides and directs, he takes full responsibility for the actions and strategies of the people he leads and if he is successful in the challenge it is because his people have acquitted themselves properly. Therefore, they are to be accorded the honours of victory, and it is the leader's responsibility to see that this is done correctly. Thus the superior man shows courage.

The inferior man cannot lead from the front. He prefers to direct affairs from a position of personal safety. He is not prepared to take the risks he asks his followers to take. He is not prepared to endanger himself personally. He is quick to receive honours which his people win, but he is not so quick to pass these honours on to his people. However it might be explained, the inferior man lacks courage in the face of his people's conviction. The superior man has no time for this sort of person.

Step Three: Hexagram 46 (The Beginning of Ascent)

The Karmic road is clear. When the time to act has come, the superior man does not hesitate. This is the time when the inferior man entertains doubts. He looks for absolute certainties, absolute guarantees. He wants to eradicate any possibility of failure before he starts. He is afraid of even the smallest risk. While the inferior man procrastinates, the superior man acts and achieves results. He makes progress at the right time.

Step Four: Hexagram 32 (Duration)

The superior man, when he is bent on achievement, knows how

to act appropriately. He contacts those people who can help him, he makes his interests known to those with whom he shares a common goal. When he is in an isolated position, he does not wait for like-minded people to seek him out. He seeks them, and thus by continuing in this way, the superior man eventually finds those people who can further him in his sphere of activity. He perseveres in this despite any setbacks or rebuffs until he is at work. The inferior man dreams about working. He thinks that people will know who he is and what he wants without him telling them, without making any effort on his part. He sits and broods in isolation. His hopes are in vain. When nothing happens, the inferior man becomes disgruntled and is easily put off even thinking about the prospect of joining with those who share an interest and a common activity. The superior man actively engages his energies in the outside world in a deliberate attempt to join with and co-operate with like-minded people.

Step Five: Hexagram 28 (Under Pressure)

The superior man, although he may be well established in his sphere of activity, encounters the ebb and flow of change just as in every other sphere of life. This is an immutable law of change. However, the superior man, when his own position is threatened, or his situation has grown old, does not cut his losses, so to speak. That is, he does not turn his back on those to whom he has pledged his loyalty and responsibility, in order to safeguard his own personal security and personal prosperity. The inferior man behaves in this way because he lacks the breadth of vision to understand his own part in the immutable cycle of change: the spring, summer, autumn and winter cycle in which one may prosper and grow poor according to the time.

An inferior man who has social standing and rank is a

danger to the stability of society because at critical moments in the cycle of change he is motivated by fear and selfishness instead of kindness and benevolence. It is because he does not understand the interrelatedness of the seasons and the interconnectedness of events that he acts in such a way as to create poor conditions for the coming season. Even in times of decay, if the seeds are not planted in time in order to sprout anew in the spring, there will be no harvest in the autumn. If the inferior man in the superior position perpetuates this from season to season, he can create a spiral of misery through generations of people by his fear of insecurity, panic to save himself, his personal greed and his total lack of foresight and understanding. Thus the law can be stated: if you contravene the Tao, untenable relationships are set up and these have dire consequences through the ages until the superior man intervenes and tunes his actions with the Tao.

Step Six: Hexagram 44 (Coming to Meet)

Sometimes, the superior man is possessed of a vision which penetrates deeply into the corruptions of a society which has adopted inferior ways as its main characteristics. He sees that there are many inferior men in superior positions. He sees that the daily lives of people are motivated by selfishness and greed and a general lack of interest in the plight of the poor and the needy. He sees inferior men rise through the ranks through nepotism, sophistry and obsequious behaviour. Everywhere he sees true and upright people downtrodden. He sees those deserving of merit neglected and unrecognised. He sees hard work go unrewarded. He sees charity abused. So it is not without justification that when the architects of this inferior way approach him, he turns his back on them and refuses to have anything whatsoever to do with them.

The superior man sees his situation as highly complex and

ambiguous as on the one hand he sees what is wrong, and on the other recognises his relative powerlessness to change things without compromising his dignity and without working with inferior men who are in superior positions. Thus he cannot ignore the plight of others, but neither can he help them. He therefore regards his own stance as a negative stance, but feels he has no other chance but to withdraw into himself until (if ever) an opportunity presents itself whereby he can make some positive contribution to change.

This was very much the attitude of Lao Tzu when he resolved to walk into the desert and die, and of Socrates when he refused to be saved from his death sentence, and of Jesus Christ who refused to answer in his own defence at his trial, and of Ghandi who was prepared to die of starvation when he truly believed that he had no other course of action when civil war broke out.

Synthesis

You have the energy and the vision to be the architect of good systems which will widely benefit others. You could, however, manifest your talents in the opposite extreme and cause much suffering for humanity. Whatever the level of society you operate within, the tendencies remain true. The most difficult Karmic lesson is to distinguish how positive and negative are manifested throughout the seasons of the year. If you can understand the interrelatedness of events, peoples and systems, and learn to plan according to the scheme, or Tao, you will avoid many harsh backlashes. Foresight is the key word in this Karmic landscape.

INNOCENCE

Hexagram 25

FOR
THOSE
BORN ON
THE 25th DAY
OF THE
MONTH

> *Your Karmic number is 25 (Heaven-oriented). The circumstances of your domestic life are vital to your overall success and personal happiness. Set yourself up in a quiet and serene neighbourhood away from the smog and smoke, noise and bustle of heavy industry and traffic. While you may enjoy frequent visits to the high energy world of the city, don't expect to flourish in it. Working from a more green environment you can adopt a more balanced view of life. As it is your tendency to be self-effacing, this can undermine very real abilities. You need to see yourself achieve before you believe in your own capabilities, and you tend to give up all too easily if your lack of belief in yourself is endorsed by others or reflected in the failure of a project. The key to your success is to believe in your own charisma at all costs and to refuse to listen to others who deliberately undermine your confidence. Once you have overcome the self-confidence crisis, you will discover that people will begin to understand you better, and this, of course, is an invitation to succeed in any field to which you are drawn. Simplicity is your watchword.*

YOUR ROOT HEXAGRAM: HEXAGRAM 25

Your root hexagram gives the climate or ambience of the six Karmic pictures which are the principal characteristics of your Karmic journey.

The import of your Karmic root is extremely simple: follow

151

the dictates of your heart. Don't look for hidden and sly motives in others, don't be sneaky or sly in yours. This hexagram is called 'Innocence' because it is about a fundamental quality of human nature. People are naturally guided by their hearts. They are naturally good, naturally innocent. It is only when we try to seek an unequal advantage over others that we become devious, and out of this tendency streams the whole gamut of nasty qualities: greed, selfishness, viciousness and so on. This observation should remain uppermost in your life as it will enable you to get a clear perspective on any situation which requires you to deal with other people.

The laws of resonance describe the way we attract and repel people. If we act without guile, this sets up a resonance (vibration) which communicates quite definitely, consciously or unconsciously, to others and invokes a like response. Do not be tempted into adopting a suspicious turn of mind when you encounter what is clearly a false resonance in response to yours. This usually means that the person in question is seeking to take advantage of your openness, but if you respond with suspicion, you set up a spiral of mutual suspicion and therefore nothing can be done; the obstacle between you becomes more dense. So long as you remain true to yourself (that is to say, fundamentally innocent of devious intentions) then you are always in a position of eventually making yourself understood even to a devious person, and therefore a successful outcome is always possible. People become all too easily afraid of being taken advantage of, and they can become obsessed with taking more and more elaborate precautions to avoid being cheated. This is why lawyers make so much money and security systems sell; they exploit the lack of trust between people, and augment further insecurity.

Step One: Hexagram 12 (Superficiality)

The picture here is of the superior man who has chosen to withdraw from the usual activities of daily life because an opportunity to make his influence felt has been denied him. He therefore considers seriously the idea of retiring — that is, of ceasing to *attempt* to make his influence felt. These thoughts are not so much chosen as forced upon him by circumstances. If he does not move in a positive direction of some kind he will lose his control over the situation. The inferior man finds this prospect highly disquieting and tries to persuade others to follow him into retirement. The superior man retires to preserve his integrity. The inferior man retires in order to hide.

Step Two: Hexagram 6 (Deadlock)

The superior and the inferior are in conflict. The inferior man will fight at all costs to preserve false pride and regardless of any damage that may be caused. The superior man recognises that in the face of a superior adversary — that is to say, an opponent who is clearly stronger — there is no shame in declining the challenge. There is no point in entering into a situation where there is no possibility of a fair fight. Where the outcome is a foregone conclusion, no purpose will be served in engaging in battle. The superior man therefore acts in a perfectly logical manner and withdraws, while the option to do so still remains open.

Step Three: Hexagram 44 (Coming to Meet)

Here the inferior man has chosen to enter into relations with other inferior people, but the superior man, employing forces beyond the comprehension of the inferior man, and against the will of the inferior man, prevents such meetings from taking place. This causes the inferior man great confusion and anxiety as he cannot see the restraining forces which inhibit his misguided intentions. The superior man recognises that his actions have saved the inferior man from the dire consequences which would have resulted had he had his own way. The inferior man, however, is completely oblivious to this line of reasoning, but is nevertheless saved from himself.

Step Four: Hexagram 57 (The Gentle (Penetrating Wind))

Over the years, the superior man accumulates a great deal of experience in handling the affairs of his life. He understands the times and is in tune with the events around him. Now that he is in a position of strength, when the opportunity to bring off a resounding success presents itself, he is even able to surprise himself, for he achieves a success three times greater than he planned for. This is the benefit of the superior man who, throughout his life, has taken careful note of the different conditions in which he has played a part and has therefore learned to read the signs with immense accuracy. Thus the superior man is able to time his actions to perfection and is able to take full advantage of the propitiousness of the times.

The inferior man cannot do this. He misses opportunity after opportunity.

Step Five: Hexagram 18 (Work on What Has Been Spoiled)

Here the superior man approaches the inferior man with the offer of help in order to put right something in the inferior man's past. Such a noble act attracts helpers and praise. Thus the superior man is able to make amends for past mistakes, and this is quite properly well received.

Step Six: Hexagram 46 (Pushing Upward)

Even when the superior man has made a great deal of progress and he has become accustomed to making such progress without any impediment for a prolonged period of time, he still keeps his eyes on the road. Placed in exactly the same predicament, the inferior man easily loses his concentration and waltzes gaily along without looking where he is going until he runs out of steam.

Furthermore, the superior man knows when a particular stretch of the road requires careful negotiation or even avoidance and because he is looking where he is going, he does not, as the inferior man would, heedlessly travel straight into a danger zone, possibly damaging himself or his vehicle. ('Vehicle' here may be a metaphor for the superior man's company, school, country, physical body, his car, ship and *ejusdem generis*.)

Synthesis

The essence of success in travelling your Karmic road is in knowing when to stop — whether this be in regard to social situations, leadership situations or any of the situations described in the Karmic pictures above, which are of course the principal ones to watch for, the story remains the same.

FOR
THOSE
BORN ON
THE 26th DAY
OF THE
MONTH

Hexagram 26

> *Your Karmic number is 26 (Earth-oriented). You have a highly developed facility for organising your resources — in fact, you are good at organising in general. You could be a philosopher or a very sharp executive. You are naturally enthusiastic, though you may conceal your enthusiasm behind the inscrutable face of caution. Your home base is critically important to you. You can be frenetic and over-anxious if you are expected to accept responsibility without a lair to return to. In fact, you might even be happier working from home because you like your creature comforts. You have an immense facility for remembering every detail of the past, but it takes great emotional stamina to be able to cope with such a prodigious memory. Images are triggers and you are always firing them off. This can create tremendous emotional turbulence and you can have a real fight holding yourself together at times. The secret of your success is finishing your projects and being unafraid of delving deeply into things.*

YOUR ROOT HEXAGRAM: HEXAGRAM 26

Your root hexagram gives the climate or ambience of the six Karmic pictures which are the principal characteristics of your Karmic journey.

Your Karmic root endows you with immense tenacity, and this is expressed in a number of valuable ways. When other people's weakness is so great that they lose control over their lives, yours is the ability to hold them together. You have immense sanity. Your character is possessed of such a fundamental strength and stability that even where others all around you might be literally losing their minds, you can be a force of such strength that you can anchor people to reality just by being yourself. Although you might in your early life feel that you are encountering problems of personal identity, all that is really happening is that you are expanding your mind. Compared to the problems of identity that some people go through, your sense of self-doubt is the equivalent of a ripple on a lake to someone else's tidal wave. It is extremely unlikely that you will ever need a psychiatrist – it is much more likely that you will be the psychiatrist, if not by profession, then through your relationships. People will naturally sense this strength in you and you may even find yourself attracted to extremely unstable people so that they can use you as a solid reference point. Never, but never, let anyone question or undermine your sanity or the integrity of your relationship with yourself in these highly personal matters because the effect could be devastating. It would be like being uprooted. Anyone who does question your sanity – your hold on reality – is likely to be imposing their own insecure identity on you. Don't be hypnotised by them.

Your influence on others will always come about through the effect of your naturally strong personality, and more often than not your influence is salubrious and calming.

Step One: Hexagram 18 (Work on What Has Been Spoiled)

The superior man endeavours to keep abreast of the times. He remains adaptable so that he can change with the times. He makes it his business to be well informed and is prepared, if necessary, to reorganise and restructure his values and commitments in order to be effective in the times in which he lives. The inferior man allows himself to slip behind the times, holds on to outmoded views and ideas. When he loses effectiveness he blames his plight on earlier generations. He sees no need to modify or radically alter his attitudes because he is not in touch with the times.

Step Two: Hexagram 52 (Learning to Relax)

The Karmic progression continues the theme of changing with the times, but here a new meaning is brought to light for the superior man. He does not allow himself to be swept along by the momentum of change with others if he feels they are misguided or moving in the wrong direction. Here is the picture of the superior man who recognises that the momentum of change is sweeping others in an inferior direction. He immediately takes action and while he is able to stop himself and change his direction to the superior way, the forces of inertia carry the others on. The superior man in such circumstances has no other choice but to go the way his heart dictates, even though he may feel a certain sadness in so doing. Nevertheless the superior man never follows an inferior path, whatever the consequences.

The inferior man is not able to make such decisions. He cannot follow his heart if this means going his own way against the crowd, and thus he shares the destiny of inferior men.

Step Three: Hexagram 23 (Separation)

The superior man following this Karmic path will encounter the difficult choice between following the path of the inferior man and following his heart: going his own way. This involves leaving behind people or an individual who are not destined to follow the same Karmic path in life. For the superior man this is an arduous but unavoidable decision and the consequences of not taking this decision would substantially diminish the power and prospects of the superior man which he can only realise by following the superior way. So difficult is this Karmic obstacle for the superior man that he may, against his own better judgment, procrastinate even for years: he may, in order to avoid making the decision, delude himself that he is able to transform the ways of the inferior man and in some way convert him to the path of the superior way. But this is never to be. These are matters of destiny for the superior man, and there is nothing he can do to change it. All he can do is yield to the unmistakable attraction he has for the superior way, though this may seem hard on those he leaves behind. In reality, he has no choice, and circumstances will repeatedly bring this to his attention until he understands it.

If the superior man misses the first opportunities to go his own way, the intensity of the inferior way will increase until he feels its malevolence so strongly that he is compelled to, as it were, break away. Thus the nature of this juncture in the Karmic road cannot be altered.

Step Four: Hexagram 35 (Progress)

The inferior man is always susceptible to offers of wealth, position and power which can be acquired by dishonest or underhand means. He will be tempted into clandestine practices and follow unwholesome methods in order to achieve what he believes are personal advantages. He will have recourse, without any kind of moral consideration, to every and any activity which serves his ends, and he will deviously try to avoid the consequences of his actions by concealing them under a cloak of secrecy. Thus the path of the inferior man is utterly reprehensible when it disguises itself as the superior path.

The superior man can see right through these designs, and he is never duped, lured, attracted into having any involvement with the ways of the inferior man. When the superior man draws close to the inferior man in this Karmic frame, the inferior man is in considerable danger, as the light of the superior man will expose him every time. Thus the inferior man cannot escape the consequences of his actions, and the downfall of the inferior man inevitably comes to pass, despite his self-deception.

Step Five: Hexagram 12 (Superficiality)

When the superior man achieves success, wealth, position and recognition, he never becomes arrogant, conceited or rests on his laurels. He works on. The inferior man, in exactly the same position, succumbs to all these personal dangers and it is always at this point that he makes the blunder that undoes him.

Step Six: Hexagram 45 (The Group)

The superior man transmits sincerity in everything he does and says. Thus other superior men recognise him for what he is. It is difficult for the superior man to be misunderstood by other superior men, therefore he need have no misgivings. Only the inferior man will misunderstand the intentions of the superior man, but even here the superior man's misgivings are entirely misplaced. It sometimes happens that an inferior man comes between two superior men and therefore brings about misunderstanding and lack of recognition between them. However, the superior way eventually overcomes the inferior way and the superior men understand each other again.

It is worth noting that the ability of the inferior man to come between superior men is among his more disgraceful qualities and can cause delays.

Synthesis

Your Karmic path will bring you some of the home comforts of the superior way, but if you get blasé and arrogant and forego the deeper considerations of your position, you will lose it all.

FOR
THOSE
BORN ON
THE 27th DAY
OF THE
MONTH

HEALTH
(BODY AND MIND)

Hexagram 27

Your Karmic number is 27 (Heaven-oriented). When you are at your most positive, your qualities are very considerable. You bear responsibility easily and well. You prefer to lead, rather than to be led. When you make decisions, you naturally take into account the whole picture. That is to say, you not only provide excellent reasons, arrived at logically, but your intuitive and psychic abilities play a large part in shaping your final decisions. Indeed, it is your sixth sense which enables you to understand and gain an enormous amount of pleasure from a very wide range of abstract ideas. You are able to be highly objective, and this is what can make a good leader. On the negative side, strongly felt emotions can undermine your objectivity, and they can be expressed as unnecessary prejudice. If you do not seek avenues in which your positive side can flourish, you tend to lose confidence and withdraw into yourself and you are very difficult to tempt out again. Beyond this, you are basically easy-going, friendly and likeable, and the very soul of modesty. You can fulfil yourself working with refined and detailed ideas though you may find it hard to work with others on this. You are more a giver than a taker.

YOUR ROOT HEXAGRAM: HEXAGRAM 27

Your root hexagram gives the climate or ambience of the six Karmic pictures which are the principal characteristics of your Karmic journey.

163

Your Karmic root hexagram is all about how to maintain a healthy equilibrium. Everything you do in life will stem from the balance you manage to achieve between a healthy mind and a healthy body. This is why the hexagram is called 'Nourishment'.

If you manage to achieve a healthy mind and a healthy body through the proper quality and measure of intake of 'food', you achieve what the *I Ching* calls 'a superior character'. The *I Ching* says: 'The superior man is careful of his words and temperate in eating and drinking'. In this way he instils into his nature a capacity for calmness and it is through the cultivation of calmness that you are able to be adaptable.

Step One: Hexagram 23 (Separation)

The Karmic picture is of the superior man whose position is undermined and threatened because he is surrounded by inferior men who are in league with each other against the superior man. This is expressed in the degrading and highly reprehensible habit of the inferior men of ganging up on the superior man, spreading nasty lies, vicious rumours and being generally deceitful and obnoxious. Under no circumstances does the superior man enter into the inferior way by retaliating, as it is the hope and the intention of the inferior men. He keeps his silence, retains his tolerance and patience, and if they press upon him he withdraws into himself. Thus the inferior men can do the superior man no harm.

The inferior man cannot understand, no matter how hard he tries, why the superior man does nothing to reply. Thus the inferior man is thrown into confusion and his capacity to do harm is substantially weakened and the danger passes.

Step Two: Hexagram 4 (The Inexperience of the Young/The Student)

The inferior man does not have enough generosity of spirit, vision or humility, to suffer fools gladly. Indeed, he is often notorious for this. But in this, he merely exhibits his bad manners, demonstrates his conceit and shows that he is not suited to positions of authority.

But here, it is the superior man who triumphs over the inferior man. Because he is in a position of responsibility and authority, he shows deference to weakness and does not run roughshod over it. Because of his lack of conceit, he is not inhibited in suffering fools gladly. Thus the superior man wins the assent of others and their co-operation.

Step Three: Hexagram 18 (Work on What Has Been Spoiled)

The superior man does not pass over past mistakes if he can correct them. Because he is determined to sweep his life clean, he can set about this with considerable energy. But perhaps he can be overzealous and create discomfort for other people.

The inferior man, motivated to make amends, tends to be lackadaisical about it, and so does not do the job properly. The superior man's position is therefore preferred, but not ideal.

Step Four: Hexagram 50 (The Cauldron/Valuable Work)

It is of great concern to the superior man when inferior men hold positions of authority for which they are not suitably endowed. Where inferior men hold superior positions, they make the wrong judgments and cause mistakes which have consequences which can spiral through generations, even centuries. The ideal position is that where superior men hold superior positions. Their authority is equal to their strength, judgment, sincerity, humility and moral rectitude. They are the true servants of the people.

The inferior man is weak, arrogant, selfish and morally embryonic. He does not wish to serve; he wishes to control. His qualities are not equal to his position. He cannot grasp the interrelatedness of events and cannot follow the consequences of his decisions into every sector of society over which he has power. He does not understand the effects of his actions.

Clearly stated here is the distinction between the ruler who serves (the superior man) and the ruler who delights in control (the inferior man). Structures which attract the latter man are tyrannous.

Step Five: Hexagram 44 (Coming to Meet)

This Karmic picture follows the theme of qualities of leadership which are so central to this Karmic number. Here the superior man is the leader and his qualities fit him properly for the job. There is no quarrel with the superior man for he controls the inferior man. Everything is in its right place. The picture of responsibility and rulership as servant and not controller is in correct focus.

The superior man is able to get things done. He is able to exercise his ability to take decisions and wins the unopposed co-operation of those whom he has the privilege to serve. His personal magnetism has full effect and there is an open and friendly atmosphere. His toleration and kindness are keenly felt, and this is as it should be.

Step Six: Hexagram 28 (Under Pressure)

The superior man pursues the superior way even if this leads him into a dangerous situation which is not of his own choosing. Usually, the superior man will avoid deliberately entering into a dangerous situation because it is foolish wilfully to court danger. However, if there is no alternative, that is, if the choice is between following the inferior way or following the superior way, the superior man will if necessary sacrifice his own life. There is no doubt that the superior man is acting correctly in such extreme circumstances.

Synthesis

You were born to be an effective and strong leader. You are naturally endowed with all the correct qualities. Your Karmic road will test your powers of leadership consistently. People will always look to you for the initiative, and you have to be ready at all times to respond to the best of your abilities. This is the nature of the contribution you will make to society if you follow your Karmic road.

FOR
THOSE
BORN ON
THE 28th DAY
OF THE
MONTH

UNDER PRESSURE

Hexagram 28

> *Your Karmic number is 28 (Earth-oriented). You are attracted to the unique, the bizarre, the unusual, and you like to work with people who are original, inventive, perhaps even strange. If you are adventurous and are prepared to take risks, you could make a good living out of the curious and the fascinating in life. Deep down, however, you are probably a traditionalist, perhaps even authoritarian. You like to know the limits of things and you like to feel supported by convention. Your aesthetic attraction is probably to things which have a symmetrical quality. Ideas and people which have a feeling of completeness about them are attractive to you. A staunch individualist yourself, you resent having your authority undermined or challenged. You don't like having your toes trodden on. You might even be afraid of commitment, or being compelled by circumstances to stick by your agreements or by decisions. Your original hunches have a way of paying off eventually and you stalk your dreams relentlessly, but you might be a waster and you are not above holding a grudge. You like to be pampered, but you might feel guilty about it.*

YOUR ROOT HEXAGRAM: HEXAGRAM 28

Your root hexagram gives the climate or ambience of the six Karmic pictures which are the principal characteristics of your Karmic journey.

Your Karmic journey is going to be much easier if you

become aware of a very powerful tendency in your nature which can be described in one word: obsession. If you apply, especially in times of transition, too much force, too much energy at a weak connection, you can lose perspective. The exact opposite of obsession as it applies to a situation of unbalanced forces, is delicacy, lightness of touch, finesse, gentleness. If you cultivate these qualities, if you wish to understand your own nature and if you wish to find the appropriate way of handling potentially overloaded situations, you must learn not to use a carving knife where a scalpel is appropriate, or your fists where the sensitive tips of your fingers are required. Not wishing to labour the point, you can only measure what is appropriate force in any given situation if you take time to put out sensitive feelers rather than rushing in unintentionally destroying things. The image is not one of clumsiness, but more the requirement for considerably more sensitivity. All this applies in exceptional circumstances, at times of great change.

Step One: Hexagram 43 (Personal Resolution)

The superior man does not stay idle when he is able to make progress, but he knows that all progress depends upon his understanding his own strength. That is to say, he does not overestimate or underestimate his own energy and power. When confronted by opposition, the inferior man who has overestimated his strength can be stopped by a superior force very early in life. The superior man never overestimates his own strength, thus he understands the idea of appropriate force. He can tune himself with his challenges. The inferior man underestimates the opposition and acts according to his imaginary power and not according to his real power. Therefore the inferior man is always in danger of coming unstuck when he is under pressure. It is possible for the superior man to test and measure his strength so that he knows what kinds of challenges he can successfully meet and what challenges are beyond him. This is the wisdom of the superior man. Only the inferior man behaves foolishly when he is confronted with an opponent whose strength is in reality unknown. It is foolish of the inferior man to assume that because the strength of his opponent is unknown it is therefore less than his own. If he is right he is fortunate, if he is wrong he is ruined. It is therefore an unwarranted risk which the superior man does not take.

Step Two: Hexagram 49 (Dynamism)

The Karmic picture is of the superior man who wishes to undergo either personal and very radical change in his attitudes, that is, he wishes to evolve himself in order to be more effective, or he wishes to change his orientation, his circumstances, his work, his perspective on life. In both cases the change is radical and far-reaching. In these circumstances the challenges to change are too strong to undertake alone. Thus the proper course for the superior man is not to attempt such a transition without the aid of a person who is known to be strong and able in this work; a person whose reputation is well respected by superior men. The superior man actively seeks this man, and does not wait to be met half-way. He knows that if the superior man helps him his transition will be successful.

The inferior man would attempt to effect such changes without the good offices of the superior man and must fail as a result as the work of transition is far too radical and far reaching for the inferior man to understand. Only a superior man can imagine what might be involved in changes of this kind, and so only a superior man can be successful in bringing them about. Thus the superior man would not attempt such a change without the help of another superior man.

Step Three: Hexagram 17 (Mutuality)

Following upon the theme of the transition of the superior man to a more integrated way of life, here the Karmic picture is of the superior man who arrives upon this new plateau of awareness. So different does the world look now that the superior man realises that in terms of his life he has made a quantum leap forward and that he has realised a better way of life which before he had only intuited was possible. The superior man has no regrets. He is fortunate in his realisation that he has finally arrived at the superior way. He has no other choice now but to follow it with determination.

The inferior man takes refuge in the wayward ideas of the past, but this is no place for such ideas.

Step Four: Hexagram 3 (Difficult Beginnings)

The superior man has no need to feel embarrassment when he seeks the help and guidance of other superior men. Other superior men understand his need and respond favourably and kindly to an attitude of open humility. The superior man need have no regrets in accepting any help from other superior men.

The inferior man, for fear of losing personal esteem, and for fear of being thought of as inferior, would never ask the superior man for anything. The inferior man is an egotist and suffers the consequences of being so. The weight of his egotistical self-opinion denies him the opportunity to be helped by the superior man. Thus the superior man avoids disgrace by welcoming and accepting the help of superior men, while the inferior man abides in disgrace for not seeking the help of the superior man.

Step Five: Hexagram 24 (Transition)

Continuing upon the theme of change and transition, this Karmic picture depicts the actual moment in which the transition is able to take place. This is the place where the inferior man reconciles himself in life to the superior man. It pictures a complete change of heart. Often the process is difficult and painful, for when the inferior man has a strong ego, he does not have an easy death. Nevertheless, the transition is clean and successful and is reflected in the arrival of the superior man in a field of action in which there is room only for superior acts. The superior man has no regrets.

Step Six: Hexagram 27 (Health)

The superior man, now completely unopposed, takes complete possession of his Karmic road. He is now a man of power and influence which can have no other effect than to bring substantial benefit to all those whom he encounters. He may act as a conduit or catalyst for people to join the superior way. He is able to accept difficult and challenging tasks and make them succeed.

Synthesis

Your Karmic road is destined to bring you into intimate contact with two very different experiences of life. You yourself will make the transition from a lower state of awareness to a higher state of awareness. Although you will not make that transition without help, you will recognise that moment as being the most significant moment of your life. From your perspective in the higher state of awareness, you can be all the more effective in helping those who are in a lower state of awareness than yourself because you yourself have been there and understand the trials and tribulations of that lower road. There are not many people who know both sides and therefore can really be of help in radically transforming society. If you have achieved the higher state of awareness, you will certainly and inevitably be attracted to superior men who share your vocation to help transform society for the better.

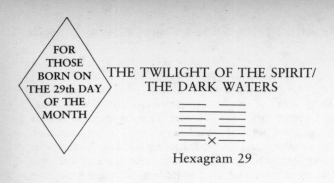

THE TWILIGHT OF THE SPIRIT/
THE DARK WATERS

Hexagram 29

> *Your Karmic number is 29 (Heaven-oriented). This is the Karmic number of those who have the power of spiritual regeneration. Depending on how well you have developed yourself spiritually, you can affect society in its extremes: you will either achieve great good or you will be the instrument of great evil. Which it is depends upon the degree of your own spiritual elevation, and to a large extent this may mean your ability to resist the temptation to abuse your talents through being motivated by greed. It is inevitable that if you nurture your abilities, you may achieve considerable recognition, even fame, and in this light, you may be asked or compelled to assume responsibilities of leadership. But you have to maintain a balance in your life. It is not enough for you to reflect or pursue your ideals in any one form of expression. You will need to develop your talents as fully as possible in some artistic or creative way in order to avoid becoming a lopsided personality. Emotional equilibrium is something you must learn to cultivate as your responsibilities increase. It may be given to you to make certain ideals realities.*

YOUR ROOT HEXAGRAM: HEXAGRAM 29

Your root hexagram gives the climate or ambience of the six Karmic pictures which are the principal characteristics of your Karmic journey.

You will come to realise that the very nature of your Karmic path is unusually dangerous. The danger is not inherent in your nature, but outside you. The first thing you have to do is accept it and get used to it, but without taking it for granted. The second situation you must note concerns your own disposition. You are the kind of person who stares long and hard at the water before jumping in. The point is to jump in anyway and not be afraid of doing so. The third thing to note is that you need have no fear that by jumping into a situation you will lose yourself. You have a natural and in-built facility for handling the most dangerous situations without coming to harm. This is not the same as an attitude of foolhardiness. The hexagram merely suggests a natural facility for coping with the situation by instinctively knowing how to behave correctly. In a sense, you have a gift for resonating with problems that seem to have no solution. Providing you jump in, you can find solutions to problems which, for other people, are completely intractable or which others are frightened to take on because for them it would be dangerous.

You are possessed of a rare quality. The *I Ching* says: '. . . once we have gained inner mastery of a problem, it will come about naturally that the action we take will succeed.' Thus all that is necessary, once the commitment has been made to solving these objective problems, is to set about the matter thoroughly and methodically and without delay.

It may be given to you to dredge up pearls of wisdom from the dark murky depths of uncharted waters unhindered and unmolested by others, simply because you are uniquely qualified to handle the peculiar dangers involved where they are not. This is why the *I Ching* says: 'Thus the superior man walks in lasting virtue and carries on the business of teaching.'

Step One: Hexagram 60 (Limitation/Discrimination)

The Karmic picture here is of the superior man who perceives the landscape stretching out before him. He has not yet embarked on his Karmic road and at the present time he is unable to do so due to certain impediments. However, these impediments are not of his own making and they will dissolve of their own accord. Thus the superior man bides his time and waits for the dissolution of the obstacles to come about. He prudently keeps his own council and stores up his energy for future action.

The inferior man, when things are at their beginning, does not have the inner calm to wait patiently, but fights obstacles in order to make a start before the time is right. But the energy is wasted because the time has not yet come to act.

The superior man does not deliberately enter into conflict with the inferior man.

Step Two: Hexagram 3 (Difficult Beginnings)

It is right for the superior man, when he confronts obstacles in his work, to welcome the help and assistance of other superior men. This Karmic picture portrays the superior man in an ambiguous predicament. In order to overcome inherently difficult situations, over which he has no control, he would like to accept the offer of help from another superior man. However, the superior man in question is not right for him. Thus the superior man learns to discriminate even among superior men and must have the wisdom in special circumstances to refuse help from another superior man, even though the help is unsought.

The destiny of the superior man is to be offered help from the right quarter further down the Karmic road. Until such time, the superior man continues to work on and does not attempt to attack these difficulties until he receives the right help, and then the difficulties are dissolved.

Step Three: Hexagram 63 (Completion)

The superior man has had a struggle to establish his position in the world, but now his achievements are recognised and he is able to draw up a more expansive scheme of action in which he can expect greater co-operation. The challenges of the future will carry their own difficulties and the superior man will have to waste less time and energy fighting off inferior influences which were his lot in the beginning. The nature of his past experience has made such a powerful impression on the superior man that he has been made to learn his lessons well in order to make the most of his expanded opportunities for action and achievement. Thus the superior man does not make the same mistakes twice. The attitude of the superior man is one of gratitude in so far as he is able to give himself more effectively to his work and with the minimum waste of energy, which up until now has been the bugbear of his life.

The inferior man, placed in a similar predicament, becomes conceited and arrogant at the grandness of his schemes and at the dizzy heights to which he has risen. These attitudes can only taint the achievements of the superior man, and therefore he wastes no time in self-glorification of any kind as this is only another form of wasting energy.

Step Four: Hexagram 49 (Dynamism)

The superior man is placed in a position of bringing about revolutionary changes. He enters upon such an office with extreme caution as he knows that radical change which is designed to affect society in general, must be based upon a clear insight into the needs of the people. Thus radical changes must bear the quality of a high standard of justice and fairness. The superior man only acts with the purest of motives as he knows that if the changes which are proposed do not relieve the needs of the people, they will instinctively reject them. If the judgments made are based upon the wrong values, a counter-revolution will result. Thus the superior man is cautious when implementing radical changes in society, as they must be designed to improve conditions for the people.

The effects of radical change must have a genuine and real benefit or they can never be justified. The changes contemplated here must go to the *roots* of the needs of people, and not merely satisfy the needs of a small section or class of society.

Step Five: Hexagram 55 (Abundance/The Brimming Cup)

The superior man at his best does not adopt an attitude of aggression. He is by nature gentle and mild. He never considers himself above seeking or accepting advice from other superior men. Since he is open in this way, and is well disposed to considering the opinions of others, he is often the recipient of new ideas which he may employ in the service of his work. The result is successful and recognised work, and often brings to the superior man substantial reward. The benefits of the work of the superior man are always passed on to those whom it will most help, and this sets up a spiral of good fortune which sets an example for others. The Tao of good fortune is implied in this dynamic. The Karma of generosity is a powerful Karma which can reach around the world.

Step Six: Hexagram 30 (Fires of the Heart)

The superior man has reached the spiritual height. Now he understands the folly of men and this brings about an expansion of awareness: this is not confined to a perceptual or conceptual breakthrough, but extends into the realm of feeling and the capacity for kindness and total understanding. This will express itself as a love for mankind as a whole, real dispassionate caring such as true leaders must be invested with.

Synthesis

Your Karmic road is difficult to start with, and if you can avoid hurting yourself too much in the early days, you will achieve, according to your energy, vision and commitment, fruitful and valuable work. The keener your concentration on the one hand and the more balanced your emotions on the other, the greater will be your achievement.

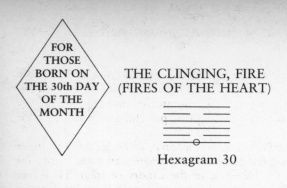

FOR
THOSE
BORN ON
THE 30th DAY
OF THE
MONTH

THE CLINGING, FIRE
(FIRES OF THE HEART)

Hexagram 30

Your Karmic number is 30 (Earth-oriented). You may not like to admit it, but you are a bit of a show-off. If you are not yourself obsessed with being the centre of attention, you might express your love of showmanship either by admiring it in others, taking photographs of it, or engaging in some kind of creative visual or musical expression. In some way you will try to stamp your mark in some visual or aural form. You live in the world of the imagination. If you are not emotionally secure, you could become paranoid and overstate everything, including yourself. Until you have a clear idea of what you want to do in life, you will hopelessly dissipate your energies and suffer from the illusion that you are doing a lot, but in fact getting nothing done. But once you have found your feet, you can express yourself with determination and tenaciousness. You certainly have a sense of humour, though sometimes it can be a bit cruel. Once you have decided you really like someone, you are generous to a fault and make a staunch and loyal friend. Loyalty is an important thing to you. You find it hard to give, but once it is committed, it is not easily withdrawn and it can emotionally scar you if it is abused. If you accept tolerance from others, you must learn to be tolerant yourself. You must make the distinction between narrow-mindedness and single-mindedness. You need variety in life. Beware of getting stuck in your ways: while you are mentally alert, and quickly form opinions, you tend to hold on to them even when they are hopelessly contradicted by experience. Keep abreast of the times.

YOUR ROOT HEXAGRAM: HEXAGRAM 30

Your root hexagram gives the climate or ambience of the six Karmic pictures which are the principal characteristics of your Karmic journey.

Everything in the universe has a force, an order, and an inner harmony. This applies not only to planets and stars in the far reaches of space but likewise in the affairs of men. Therefore the limits to action, the boundaries of possibilities, are in this special sense already set. If you acknowledge and recognise that all your possibilities are dependent on existing forces, that is to say, you do not fight the thing that nurtures you, you can achieve what the *I Ching* calls 'an attitude of compliance'. This means that you accept your cosmic position in relation to your personal possibilities in life willingly, even though you have no choice, as you could not anyway change your cosmic position by fighting it. Such an alignment of attitude will enable you to perceive the obstacles in your life as nothing other than your resistance to things you cannot change. Once you have worked this out, it is possible for you to burn brightly. This is why the hexagram is called 'The Clinging, Fire'. A flame is dependent for its brightness on the matter which it burns. That is to say, you use the limitation to express your brightness. The hardest thing for you to do is to surrender yourself to the flow of things. Until you do you will achieve nothing. While this is true of people generally, and at some point in everyone's life this is something that must be learned, here it is something which is a precondition of your effectiveness and so it must be emphasised.

Step One: Hexagram 56 (The Traveller)

The superior man who finds himself travelling in foreign parts does not expect to be able to gain a deep understanding of the needs and interests of the societies which are his hosts. Therefore he does not meddle in their affairs, neither does he pretend to insights he does not possess. Therefore he does not offer commitments he has no intention of honouring, or solutions to problems which betray a superficial understanding. These faults are the province of the inferior man who quickly makes himself a burden on his hosts. The superior man, when he is travelling, is respectful of the cultures of others and does not impose his views uninvited.

Step Two: Hexagram 50 (The Cauldron/Valuable Work)

The Karmic picture depicts a superior man engaged in work which bears a distinctly spiritual hallmark. The superior man knows the value of the work, and therefore makes sure that he is not distracted so that he is able to complete it. The inferior man does not complete the work and therefore it can make no contribution to the lives of others. Thus we have a conflict between the inferior and the superior men. The work that the superior man completes is successful and well-received, though it will certainly arouse jealousy and resentment among inferior men, though this will not harm the superior man.

The inferior man who does not complete work may fall in with the way of other inferior men, and is numbered among those who are jealous and resentful. Because the inferior man passes up the opportunity of reconciling himself to the superior way, he cannot hope to cover up his deficiencies behind an attitude of mocking arrogance. The superior man is unimpressed by such displays. The only course of action for the inferior man is to regain contact with the superior man by cultivating an attitude of genuine humility.

Step Three: Hexagram 64 (Before Completion)

The superior man is always in tune with himself and in tune with the times. He therefore understands that, in the progression of changes which characterise the events of the outside world, there are specific moments when action is imperative. When the opportunity for decisive action, which will enable the superior man to progress, has come, he is fearless and does not hesitate. He acts immediately. Since we are speaking here of a major transition in the life of the superior man from one field of action to another, these important junctures must be seized as they recur only at cyclic intervals. If this opportunity is missed, another opportunity will present itself but the time will have been lost. Thus the only way to be sure of grasping the opportunity at the right time is for the superior man to be completely objective about his situation.

The inferior man fails to grasp opportunities because he is not prepared and his unpreparedness is directly related to his lack of objectivity. That is to say, he does not take his predicament in life seriously enough to engage his energies as if it mattered.

Step Four: Hexagram 4 (The Inexperience of the Young)

Without a clearly defined artistic or creative structure, wild imaginings, daydreams and fantasies lead the inferior man into dangerous waters. By constantly indulging in wayward, undirected thoughts, the inferior man loses track of himself. He becomes disoriented, confused, and he needs prominent landmarks in his personal experience by which to regain his bearings. Such a tendency can cost the inferior man valuable time and energy.

However, the superior man uses the imaginative facility in a structured way. That is to say, he creates forms and objects and colours them in with his imagination. He does not become the servant of the process. He is the master of it. Therefore he never loses his way. He keeps the whole picture in his mind and therefore he can act with purpose because he knows what he wants to achieve. The inferior man is enslaved by his imagination because he has no strategy.

Step Five: Hexagram 59 (Dissolution)

It is the Karma of the inferior man who has lost his way to wander seemingly haphazardly into the great darkness, the shadowy midnight world of the soul. Here the inferior man will find all his fears, and with his active imagination, he will paint them in garish colours and succeed in terrifying himself. The process, however, teaches a great deal, and the experience bears a great gift. First, the inferior man will realise that such a great darkness is perfectly real and not a figment of his imagination. It is a quality that exists in the world and therefore he will never, for the rest of his life, take it for granted or speak lightly of the experience; second, he will realise how insignificant and helpless he is without the light of the superior man. The immensity of the darkness is overwhelming and he will find the experience extremely uncomfortable. It is like a waking nightmare.

This is the experience which teaches the inferior man the extent of his inferiority. However, continuing on his journey, he must eventually come to the one single point of light that exists in all the darkness. This is the key to his enlightenment, both literally and figuratively, for now he sees within himself and within the world, the reality of an illuminating idea which has the effect of banishing the darkness. If he can embrace this idea, he can redeem himself out of the darkness back into the light. Since this is part of the Tao of things, it is impossible for anyone to be perpetually in darkness, as there is a seed of light in every darkness, and a lost consciousness is naturally attracted to it, as that seed of light is also within himself. Thus illusory ideas which have preoccupied and obsessed the inferior man, fall away and real understanding of his place in the scheme of things begins to emerge. The inferior man is finally reconciled with the superior man, and this is his salvation.

Step Six: Hexagram 29 (Twilight of the Spirit)

This is a picture of the inferior man's consciousness lost in a sea of darkness. Since he has lost his bearings and is floating aimlessly in inner space, the natural laws of magnetism take hold. Slowly but surely the superior man, as it were, tracks the inferior man and draws him in. The inferior man, however, is completely oblivious as to what is happening as his experience is of lostness and desolation. The wider picture is much more positive than the inferior man, in his desolate situation, can possibly imagine. He is only suffering from an illusion of lostness in the wider scheme of things, though the actual experience is, for him, quite real.

Synthesis

Your Karmic paths lead you to experiences which compel an acknowledgment of the reality of spiritual reality. So long as you do not understand your place in the wider scheme of things, you will attract to yourself those lessons which teach best. It is a matter of individual disposition how intense these spiritual lessons will be. If your nature is to be self-obsessive, egocentric, blasé, know-it-all, arrogant, the spiritual lesson will be harsh (like being purged in the Fires of the Heart); if you are highly impressionable and imaginative and even misuse mind-expanding drugs, you could really frighten yourself, and may need to place yourself under the care of spiritually knowledge-able teachers. When you have become integrated and stable you will learn the value of being objective and strategic about your life, though this does not mean being sneaky and underhand. The emphasis is upon focus and defined purpose.

INFLUENCE/
NATURAL ATTRACTION

FOR
THOSE
BORN ON
THE 31st DAY
OF THE
MONTH

Hexagram 31

Your Karmic number is 31 (Heaven-oriented). You have a very practical turn of mind. You might be good at making things. You appreciate the work that goes into building things. You have an eye for line and form — this might be expressed in a love of certain kinds of architecture and design ideas. Certainly, being involved in the structure and appearance of objects is something for which you have a marked talent. The four-square solidity of buildings is also reflected in your nature. You feel best when the foundations of your family, ideas, projects are completely secure and solid. Wishy-washy half commitments give you the creeps. Because you like close and detailed work, you do not tend to be the egocentric type — you don't spend a lot of time worrying about lofty ambitions. You tend to make steady progress and find yourself, almost unexpectedly, in a position of strength, but you are not consciously out to compete with anyone else in particular, except perhaps yourself. You are good to your friends, providing you choose them, but you might be reluctant to change with the times. You feel safer with solid, established ideas, so you are not one for taking too many chances on the new and exciting. You probably have a very close affinity with nature and if things go wrong or you have any kind of problem, you prefer to find your answers in nature rather than trust to some new-fangled remedy that comes in a bottle.

YOUR ROOT HEXAGRAM: HEXAGRAM 31

Your root hexagram gives the climate or ambience of the six Karmic pictures which are the principal characteristics of your Karmic journey.

This root hexagram is chiefly concerned with your dealings with others: your ability to influence others, and the ability of others to influence you. To take the latter influence first, avoid being too set in your opinions, or over-sure that you know what is best in every situation that arises. While it is not denied that you may well be the best person to judge, you should still keep an open mind so that you can be receptive to opinions which may be able to perfect your judgment.

The first kind of influence, your influence over others, emanates principally from a basically cheerful disposition. When you are most successful it is usually when you put a smile on for the world. But the *I Ching* emphasises that behind the smile is a peaceful heart and herein lies the power of your influence. When both these elements are present we have a picture of a charismatic person, who is able to influence others without even trying. As a matter of interest, concealed within these dynamics are the secrets of social attraction and the dynamics of empathy which are properly the subjects of hexagrams 31 to 64 of the *I Ching*.

Step One: Hexagram 49 (Dynamism)

The superior man keeps in touch with the times in which he is living. He is neither stagnant nor resistant to change, nor does he force changes to occur for which the time is not ripe. He is content to keep in tune with the season, and therefore does not go to extremes. The inferior man can easily become agitated and is not content to tune with the natural changes of the

seasons, therefore it is difficult for the inferior man to feel calm
in his daily life. The superior man, by keeping in touch with the
natural flow of the seasons, is able to keep in touch with
himself. For people who live in the city it is very difficult to
keep in touch with the natural seasons because the city
structure, to a large extent, excludes nature and natural life.
City dwellers very easily fall out of synchronisation with nature
as there is very little reflection of nature's processes in their
environment. Tension therefore becomes a problem.

Step Two: Hexagram 43 (Resolution)

The superior man develops his awareness in such a way that he
is alert to his environment. Therefore he does not live in fear of
any danger that might threaten. This is the secret. By being
cautious about the forces in his environment, but at the same
time fearless, danger cannot approach him without his knowing
about it well in advance; if the source of the danger comes into
close proximity to the superior man, it will recognise that he is
fearless and is much more likely to keep away. A predator is
attracted to fear and is repelled by fearlessness. Blind
fearlessness, however, is merely bravado and does not repel the
danger. It is aware fearlessness which repels danger. The
inferior man may be full of bravado, but his eyes and ears are
not tuned to his environment and so danger can creep up
behind him and take him by surprise. In a situation like this,
the inferior man's bravado is of absolutely no use to him.
Accordingly, the inferior man may be cautious and constantly
on the lookout for danger, but if in his heart he is terrifed of it,
then the danger is all the more attracted to him, and the
inferior man is once again vulnerable. Thus, as is pictured here,
the superior man has developed himself to the point where both
elements, alertness and fearlessness, are naturally present, so
that he can live calmly even in the midst of danger.

Step Three: Hexagram 58 (Friendship)

The Karmic picture here continues the theme of vulnerability, but this time the experience is spiritual and emotional in nature. The inferior man who is out of touch with nature, the seasons, or the Tao, feels disconnected in some cosmic sense (or is it some local sense inside his own head?) which corresponds in him with a feeling of hollowness or meaninglessness. He feels vacant and empty. Sometimes the superior man is able to clear his mind of cluttered ideas and thoughts in order to tune himself with nature, but here the inferior man experiences the exact opposite. It is rather a feeling of desolation than a positive act of tuning.

The superior man chooses to empty himself. For the inferior man, emptiness creeps up on him, and in this there is danger, for the natural tendency is for emptiness to fill itself. For the inferior man, this might quite literally take the form of alcohol. He fills himself with anything that comes to hand — it could be food, drugs — he wants to drive away the emptiness by driving himself senseless with whatever is most easily available. Taken to extremes over many years, such a tendency could have a vastly debilitating effect, as it represents an habitualised avoidance of confronting the recurring feeling of emptiness. And in this particular Karmic progression, the tendency to destroy the feeling of emptiness by over-eating or drinking to excess, which can run the body down, is in conflict with the desire to maintain vigorous health.

The crux of the issue is that there must be a balance between spiritual health and physical health. Here, spiritual ill-health, that is, not being able to cope with the feeling of emptiness or desolation, is compensated for by a process which slowly destroys the body and the mind. When both these elements are out of tune, a spiral of physical and spiritual decay is set up. The superior man cultivates that feeling of emptiness as a means of tuning to himself and his environment. The inferior man misunderstands the feeling and tries to compensate for it.

The superior man meditates, the inferior man drinks or eats or tries to lose himself in something else.

It is worth noting that in modern, western society and possibly in the rest of the world, the Karmic picture presented above describes a very common situation which has grown to such endemic proportions that it is now regarded as a social problem which threatens the cohesion of society as a whole. Since we are not talking about food and drink in their proper place, but where they are misused as an emotional crutch or to compensate for a feeling of emptiness, this does seem to indicate that we need to go beyond analysing the wholefood content or lack of content in our daily diet and teach people how to meditate as a fundamental educational requirement in society. It is my belief that meditation should be taught in both primary and secondary schools along with other compulsory subjects. Only when meditation becomes an intrinsic part of our educational process are we going to make any real sense out of our concern for physical health which has its roots in our spiritual well-being. Indeed, if modern society is to evolve, I don't think we have any choice.

Step Four: Hexagram 60 (Limitation)

When the superior man wants to achieve something, he clearly defines his field of action; he deliberately constructs guidelines and calls these the limits of his activity. He does this so that his energies are not wasted on inconsequential matters which are not germane to his defined task. He prepares his objectives thoroughly in order to make the most economical use of his energies and to maximise the effect of his efforts. But he does not over restrict his field of action so that he feels uncomfortable. He tries to find exactly the right balance so that he is able to get what he wants done with the available energy without wasting unnecessary time and effort. With practice, the superior man does this quite naturally. He need make no conscious effort as he is in tune with the work. This is the meaning of the idea of Zen in action: the art of hitting the mark with the appropriate energy by an act of tuning.

The inferior man either gives himself too much room, and thereby gets nothing finished, or gives himself too little room and becomes so frustrated that he does not want to do the work anyway.

Step Five: Hexagram 19 (The Open Door)

The act of reforming or disarming harmful personal habits and traits is the act of the superior man. A resolution to set about this kind of work attracts the help of other superior men because it assists the superior man in every other department of his life.

Step Six: Hexagram 41 (External Poverty)

The Karmic picture depicts a superior man who has cultivated his superiority to such an extent that he has achieved considerable good fortune and his superiority in the midst of his good fortune excels still further in his willingness to share it with others. The disposition of the superior man creates such a powerful and favourable impression on others that they are ready and willing to co-operate with his ideas and projects and this sets up a spiral of excellent Karma on the superior way.

Synthesis

Your Karmic road can be relatively tranquil and trouble-free if you regularly practise the art of tuning with nature through meditation. Only in this way will you be able to control any tendency to compensate for what is clearly your most vulnerable weakness: cosmic insecurity. Although it may sound incredible, your biggest fear is that your life, no matter what you put into it, may not amount to a hill of beans. Nobody can really convince anybody that life is intrinsically meaningful. It is something that has to be experienced personally and consistently if it is to be understood. A few moments spent in some meditative discipline on a daily basis will train your spiritual faculties and will provide you with the emotional and spiritual tools with which to overcome the central weakness.

EPILOGUE
The Wider Significance of the Doctrine of Karma in the I Ching

Karma is the *journey*. Fate, in the terms described herein, is the *destiny*. The Principle of Opposites from which the transformation of the actual frames derives extends also into *World Karma*. If the individual's journey to his higher self is prescribed in each life and 'the way' the individual meets his fate within those prescribed *contextual* limitations is a matter of choice, then a change in the condition of the world – *the human condition* – is not outside our collective responsibility. The existence of starvation, disease, war, and the social and political evils which beset the planet are not matters of Fate, they are matters of Karma, matters subject to collective human challenge. We cannot, therefore, disclaim responsibility, as individuals, for those events which fall under the control of human choice, whereby people can determine the quality of their lives and the lives of others.

According to the system set out here rationalising the Tao of Karma, it is possible to delineate the specific World Karmic challenges and to demonstrate how, on a global scale, it might be possible to meet these collective challenges in the light of qualitative goals and aspirations. This idea is represented in the *I Ching* as *Crossing the Great Water*. The idea of World Karma, or *collective challenge*, should now be in the forefront of political consideration. Never before in the history of mankind has there been the capacity as well as the need to reorganise global priorities for the general well-being and happiness of all peoples.

Not everyone will agree with my assumption that it may be possible to set up a fundamental basis of world integration, not as a 'philosophically desirable state of affairs', but according to the principles of Tao, i.e. flowing with the cosmic laws. That there is a cosmic logic demonstrable in scientific terms which defines the frames of choice not only for the individual but also on a far larger universal scale, is a concept to be explored further. If we knew objectively:

(a) how to understand these cosmic laws (their terms of reference) and
(b) how to apply them to the *choices* we have to make within a set of options or limits (the *frame*)

we would begin to see that there is a scheme, a Tao, and how we relate to it and evolve through it. In the *Great Treatise* we read: '. . . But movement and change come about only because the forces acting as pairs of opposites, without concealing each other, set going the cyclic movement on which the life of the world depends.' Such fundamental principles can be extended into the realm of everyday human experience, and be seen to be logical and meaningful throughout the whole consideration of the evolution of human consciousness. Rilke, in his *Requiem*, says:

> The big words from those ages when as yet
> happening was visible are not for us.
> Who talks of victory? To endure is all.

We can endure best by understanding *how*, and perhaps *why* everything connects the way it does. We must become conscious, increasingly, until as individuals and as collectivities of individuals we can make the *cosmically logical* choices. This is the fundamental Karmic Challenge which all humanity now faces at the time of the Millennium. The call is out and the right way is now becoming clearly explained and demonstrated *as law* which *transcends* all world ideologies.

Now we must find our way to discovering all of these laws and of translating them into political, social, organisational and, vitally, *economically* imperative systems. I believe humanity's future – now closer, and most alive will live to experience it – will certainly surprise, if not shock, us all. We *must* be ready.

Further Reading

Bentov, I. (1978), *Stalking the Wild Pendulum*, Hounslow, Wildwood House.

Castenada, C. (1970), *The Teachings of Don Juan*, Harmondsworth, Penguin.

Castenada, C. (1972), *A Separate Reality*, Harmondsworth, Penguin.

Castenada, C. (1974), *The Journey to Ixtlan*, Harmondsworth, Penguin.

Castenada, C. (1976), *Tales of Power*, Harmondsworth, Penguin.

Castenada, C. (1979), *The Second Ring of Power*, Harmondsworth, Penguin.

Castenada, C. (1981), *The Eagle's Gift*, Harmondsworth, Penguin.

Castenada, C. (1984), *The Fire From Within*, Harmondsworth, Penguin.

Damian-Knight, G. (1984), *The I Ching on Love*, Poole, Blandford Press.

Damian-Knight, G. (1987), *The I Ching Compass*, London, Rider Books. Here I explore the implications of unitive knowledge arising from the structures of the *I Ching*.

Hesse, Hermann (1972), *The Glass Bead Game*, Harmondsworth, Penguin.

Kwok Man Ho, Peter and Palmer, Martin (1986), *The Fortune-Teller's I Ching*, London, Rider Books. A new mathematical and interpretative evaluation of the *I Ching*.

Lao Tzu (1973), *The Tao Te Ching*, Hounslow, Wildwood House.

Ouspensky, P.D. (1986), *The Fourth Way*, London, Arkana.

Pagels, H. (1983), *The Cosmic Code*, London, Michael Joseph.

Silo (1982), *The Internal Landscape*, New York, Weiser.

Steinbrecher, E. (1982), *The Inner Guide Meditation*, Wellingborough, Aquarian Press.

Wei, Henry (1982), *The Guiding Light of Lao Tzu*, London, Quest.

Wilhelm, R. (trans.) (1968), *I Ching, or Book of Changes*, London, Routledge & Kegan Paul.

Wilson, R.A. (1979), *The Cosmic Trigger*, London, Sphere.

The Bhagavad Gita (any translation).